MA... OR
LESS ABLE
LEARNERS

- Tricky topics covered
- Ideas to build confidence
- Photocopiable activities

AGES
9

Ian Gardner

Credits

Author
Ian Gardner

Editor
Sally Gray

Assistant Editor
Catherine Gilhooly

Illustrations
Andy Robb

Series Designer
Catherine Mason

Designer
Catherine Mason

Text © Ian Gardner
© 2006 Scholastic Ltd

Designed using Adobe InDesign

Published by Scholastic Ltd
Villiers House
Clarendon Avenue
Leamington Spa
Warwickshire CV32 5PR

www.scholastic.co.uk

Printed by Bell and Bain Ltd, Glasgow.

1 2 3 4 5 6 7 8 9   6 7 8 9 0 1 2 3 4 5

British Library Cataloguing-in-Publication Data
A catalogue record for this book is available from the British Library.

ISBN 0-439-965-209
ISBN 978-0439-965200

The right of Ian Gardner to be identified as the author of this work has been asserted by him in accordance with the Copyright, Designs and Patents Act 1988.

Extracts from The National Numeracy Strategy © Crown copyright. Reproduced under the terms of HMSO Guidance Note 8.

Due to the nature of the web, the publisher cannot guarantee the content or links of any of the websites referred to. It is the responsibility of the reader to assess the suitability of websites.

Every effort has been made to trace copyright holders for the works reproduced in this book, and the publishers apologise for any inadvertent omissions.

Contents

About the series

50 Maths Lessons for Less Able Learners is a series of three books designed for teachers and learning support assistants working with lower ability children within the daily maths lesson. Each book covers a two-year span of the primary age range: KS1 5–7 and KS2 7–9 and 9–11.

Each title consists of 50 oral and mental starter activities and 50 lesson plans each with an accompanying photocopiable activity page. The activities cover many of the key objectives in the National Numeracy Strategy's Framework for Teaching Mathematics.

The lesson plans and accompanying photocopiable activities are designed to:
● Support less confident learners with a range of key mathematical concepts
● Motivate children with engaging activities and games
● Suggest ways to modify activities to address different learning styles
● Fit into the individual teacher's existing planning for mathematics.

How to use this book

This book begins with a detailed objectives grid, which gives an overview of the objectives addressed by each lesson. Teachers can also use this grid to track backwards to identify appropriate objectives from previous years where necessary.

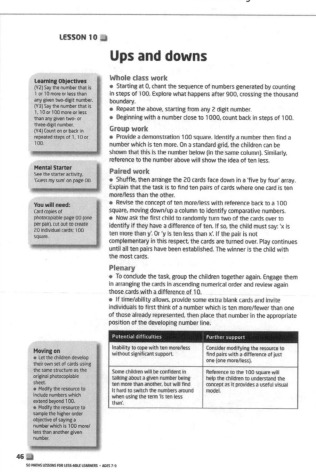

A bank of 50 oral and mental starters has then been included. Links to appropriate starters are made on each lesson plan. However, they can also be used flexibly as required. They might also be used as focused oral assessment activities with small groups. A set of target questions has been given for this purpose.

To make the book easy to use all 50 lesson plans follow the same format.

Learning objectives

Each lesson is written to address one or more of the NNS objectives from either Years 2, 3 or 4. The grid at the front of the book tracks back to show how an objective tracks back in Year 2.

Starter activity

A suggested linked mental starter activity from the bank of starters at the front of the book (pages 10–26).

Whole class work

Introduces the context and concept of each lesson to the whole class.

Group work

This details the teaching activity to be undertaken by groups of less able learners, led by either the class teacher or a teaching assistant. Various teaching strategies are used, and knowledge and skills are presented creatively to engage children and appeal to different learning styles. Opportunities for children to talk about their work and to explain their ideas and understanding are offered throughout. Activities are designed to build on what children know – the aim being to build confidence. Emphasis is placed on active participation by the children through the use of games, role play and so on. Suggested questions and opportunities for teacher interventions are also included (see below for further information).

Independent/paired work

Where appropriate an individual or paired activity is suggested. These provide opportunities for the less confident children to work with greater independence. The activities suggested are intended to reinforce and consolidate the learning that takes place in the teacher-led part of the lesson and include a variety of games, reinforcement activities or problems to solve. Many of the activities can be easily adapted to use on more than one occasion.

Plenary

Where possible the plenary offers an opportunity to reflect on less confident children's understanding of the lesson objective.

Potential difficulties and further support

This grid outlines potential difficulties children might experience. Suggestions for further differentiating the activities for children who require extra support are provided, as well as notes on adapting the activities for children's different learning styles.

Moving on

At the end of each plan ideas are included for how to extend children who have met the objectives.

Interventions

The NNS suggests that 'as far as possible, children should work together'. This inclusive approach therefore requires a variety of intervention techniques for children working significantly below expected levels of attainment. The NNS identifies three waves of possible interventions, as outlined above. These include whole class teaching for all children (wave 1), interventions in small groups with the teacher or learning support assistants (wave 2) and targeted interventions with individuals (wave 3). The lessons in this book reflect this approach with opportunities for different types of intervention offered throughout.

The *50 Maths Lessons for Less Able Learners* series sits comfortably within the principles underpinning aspects of 'Excellence and Enjoyment' (DfES, 2004), giving renewed emphasis to matters of inclusive practice and flexible curriculum planning.

Ofsted's report for 2002 confirmed that the National Numeracy Strategy continues to have a positive impact on the teaching of pupils with special educational needs. Their report also confirms that almost all pupils with special educational needs are included in the daily mathematics lesson.

The *50 Maths Lessons* series features numerous activities that call on the child to apply knowledge and understanding to wider contexts, but within an environment tailored more to the needs of the less confident learner. Through skilful and timely intervention the child is likely to be well placed to benefit from this modified programme. At the same time, the incorporation of common themes and whole class activity minimises the possibility of the child feeling excluded or marginalised.

Title of lesson	Tracking back Year 2 objectives	Year 3 objectives	Tracking forwards Year 4 objectives
1 Count me in!	● Count reliably up to 100 objects by grouping them.	● Count larger collections by grouping them: for example, in tens, then other numbers.	
2 Takes and adders!	● **Count on or back in ones or tens, starting from any two-digit number.**	● **Count on or back in tens or hundreds, from any two- or three-digit number.**	● Recognise/extend number sequences formed by counting from any number in steps of constant size, extending beyond zero when counting back: eg, count on in steps of 25 to 500, then back to, 100.
3 Odds and evens	● Count on in twos from and back to zero or any small number, and recognise odd and even numbers to at least 30.	● **Count on or back in twos from any two-digit number**, and recognise odd and even numbers to at least 100.	● Recognise odd and even numbers up to 1000, and their properties, including the outcome of sums or differences of pairs of odd/ even numbers.
4 Step by step	● Count on in steps of 3, 4 or 5 to at least 30, from and back to zero, then from and back to any given small number.	● Count on in steps of 3, 4 or 5 from any small number to at least 50, then back again.	● Know by heart facts for the 2, 3, 4, 5 and 10 multiplication tables.
5 Cover up	● Begin to recognise two-digit multiples of 2, 5 or 10.	● Recognise two-digit and three-digit multiples of 2, 5 or 10, and three-digit multiples of 50 and 100.	● Know by heart facts for the 2, 3, 4, 5 and 10 multiplication tables.
6 Hundred up	● **Read and write whole numbers to at least 100** in figures and words.	● **Read and write whole numbers to at least 1000** in figures and words.	● Read and write whole numbers to at least 10,000 in figures and words, and know what each digit represents.
7 Top totals	● Know what each digit in a two-digit number represents, including zero as a place holder, and partition two-digit numbers into a multiple of ten and ones (TU).	● Know what each digit represents, and partition three-digit numbers into a multiple of 100, a multiple of ten and ones (HTU).	● Multiply or divide any integer up to 1000 by10 (whole-number answers), and understand the effect.
8 More or less?	● Use and begin to read the vocabulary of comparing and ordering numbers, including ordinal numbers to 100. Use the = sign to represent equality.	● Read and begin to write the vocabulary of comparing and ordering numbers, including ordinal numbers to at least 100.	● Read and write the vocabulary of comparing and ordering numbers. **Use symbols correctly, including less than (<), greater than (>), equals (=).**
9 Higher...lower!	● Compare two given two-digit numbers, say which is more or less, and give a number which lies between them.	● Compare two given three-digit numbers, say which is more or less, and give a number which lies between them.	● Give one or more numbers lying between two given numbers and order a set of whole numbers less than 10,000.
10 Ups and downs	● Say the number that is 1 or 10 more or less than any given two-digit number.	● Say the number that is 1, 10 or 100 more or less than any given two- or three-digit number.	● Count on or back in repeated steps of 1, 10 or 100.
11 Take three	● **Order whole numbers to at least 100**, and position them on a number line and 100 square.	● **Order whole numbers to at least 1000**, and position them on a number line.	Read/ write the vocabulary of comparing/ordering numbers. **Use symbols correctly, including less than (<), greater than (>), equals (=).**
12 In its place	● Use and begin to read the vocabulary of estimation and approximation; give a sensible estimate of at least 50 objects.	● Read and begin to write the vocabulary of estimation and approximation.	● Read/write vocabulary of estimation and approximation. Make/justify estimates up to 250. Estimate a proportion.
13 Round up?	● Round numbers less than 100 to the nearest 10.	● Round any two-digit number to the nearest 10 and any three-digit number to the nearest 100.	● Round any positive integer less than 1000 to the nearest 10 or 100.

Title of lesson	Tracking back Year 2 objectives	Year 3 objectives	Tracking forwards Year 4 objectives
14 Bits and pieces	● Begin to recognise and find one half and one quarter of shapes and small numbers of objects.	● **Recognise unit fractions such as 1/2, 1/3, 1/4, 1/5, 1/10, and use them to find fractions of shapes and numbers.**	● Identify two simple fractions with a total of 1 (eg 3/10 and 7/10).
15 Words worth	● Extend understanding of the operations of addition and subtraction. Use and begin to read the related vocabulary.	● Extend understanding of the operations of addition and subtraction, read and begin to write the related vocabulary.	● Consolidate understanding of relationship between + and -.
16 Which way now?	● Understand that more than two numbers can be added.	● Extend understanding that more than two numbers can be added.	● Add 3 or 4 small numbers, finding pairs totalling 10, or 9 or 11. ● Add three two-digit multiples of 10, such as 40 + 70 + 50.
17 Families	● **Understand that subtraction is the inverse of addition** (subtraction reverses addition).	● Extend understand that subtraction is the inverse of addition.	● Understand the principles (not the names) of the commutative and associative laws as they apply or not to addition and subtraction.
18 Full score	● **Know by heart all addition and subtraction facts for each number to at least 10.** ● Recall all pairs of numbers with a total of 20 (eg 13 + 7, 6 + 14).	● **Know by heart all addition and subtraction facts for each number to 20.**	● Consolidate knowing by heart addition and subtraction facts for all numbers to 20.
19 Round we go	● Know by heart all pairs of multiples of 10 with a total of 100 (eg 30 + 70).	● Derive quickly all pairs of multiples of 5 with a total of 100 (eg 35 + 65).	● Derive quickly all number pairs that total 100 (eg 62 + 38, 75 + 25, 40 + 60); all pairs of multiples of 50 with a total of 1000 (eg 850 + 150).
20 Top up	● **Use knowledge that addition can be done in any order to do mental calculations more efficiently.**	● Use knowledge that addition can be done in any order to do mental calculations more efficiently.	● **Use known number facts and place value to add or subtract mentally, including any pair of two-digit whole numbers.**
21 Break it down	● Partition additions into tens and units, then recombine.	● Partition into '5 and a bit' when adding 6, 7, 8 or 9 (eg 47 + 8 = 45 + 2 + 5 + 3 = 50 + 5 = 55).	● Partition into tens and units, adding the tens first.
22 More than double	● Identify near doubles, using doubles already known (eg 8 + 9, 40 + 41).	● Identify near doubles, using doubles already known (eg 80 + 81).	● Identify near doubles, using known doubles (eg 150 + 160).
23 Ups and downs	● Add/subtract 9 or 11: add/subtract 10 and adjust by 1. Begin to add/subtract 19 or 21: add/ subtract 20 and adjust by 1.	● **Add and subtract mentally a 'near multiple of 10' to or from a two-digit number.**	● Add or subtract the nearest multiple of 10, then adjust.
24 Spot the pattern	● Use patterns of similar calculations.	● Use patterns of similar calculations.	● **Use known number facts and place value to add or subtract mentally, including any pair of two-digit whole numbers.**
25 How much?	● Use known number facts and place value to add/subtract mentally.	● Use known number facts and place value to add/subtract mentally.	● **Use known number facts and place value to add or subtract mentally, including any pair of two-digit whole numbers.**
26 Windows	● **Understand the operation of multiplication as repeated addition or as describing an array.** ● Read and begin to write the related vocabulary.	● Extend understanding that multiplication can be done in any order.	● Extend understanding of the operations of x and ÷, and their relationship to each other and to + and –.

Title of lesson	Tracking back Year 2 objectives	Year 3 objectives	Tracking forwards Year 4 objectives
27 Double trouble	● **Know and use halving as the inverse of doubling.**	● Understand division as grouping (repeated subtraction) or sharing. Read and begin to write the related vocabulary.	● Round up or down after division, depending on the context.
28 Moving on	● Know by heart doubles of all number to 10 and the corresponding halves. ● **Know and use halving as the inverse of doubling.**	● **Recognise that division is the inverse of multiplication**, and that halving is the inverse of doubling.	● Extend understanding of the operations of x and ÷, and their relationship to each other and to + and –.
29 Your call	● **Know by heart multiplication facts for the 2-times tables.**	● Know by heart multiplication facts for the 2-times tables.	● Know by heart multiplication facts for 2, 3, 4, 5 and 10 times tables.
30 Find a partner	● Derive quickly multiplication facts for the 5-times table. ● Know by heart multiplication facts for the 10-times table.	● Know by heart multiplication facts for the 5 and 10-times tables.	● Know by heart multiplication facts for 2, 3, 4, 5 and 10-times tables.
31 Links	● Count on in steps of 3, 4 or 5 to at least 30, from and back to zero.	● Begin to know the 3 and 4-times tables.	● Know by heart multiplication facts for 2, 3, 4, 5 and 10-times tables.
32 Seeing double	● Derive quickly doubles of all numbers to at least 15 (eg 11 + 11 or 11 x 2).	● Derive quickly doubles of all whole numbers to at least 20 (eg 17 + 17 or 17 x 2).	● Derive quickly doubles of all whole numbers to 50 (eg 38 + 38, or 38 x 2).
33 Double vision	● Derive quickly doubles of multiples of 5 to 50 (eg 20 x 2 or 35 x 2).	● Derive quickly doubles of multiples of 5 to 100 (eg 75 x 2, 90 x 2).	● Derive quickly doubles of multiples of 10 to 500 (eg 460 x 2).
34 Ten tens	● Derive quickly halves of multiples of 10 to 100 (eg half of 70).	● Derive quickly all the corresponding halves (eg 36 ÷ 2, half of 130, 900 ÷ 2).	● Derive quickly doubles of multiples of 100 to 5000 (eg 3400 x 2); and the corresponding halves (eg 74 ÷ 2, 1/2 of 420, half of 3800).
35 Work it out	● Use known number facts and place value to carry out mentally simple multiplications and divisions.	● Use doubling or halving, starting from known facts (eg 8 x 4 is double 4 x 4).	● Use doubling or halving, starting from known facts. For example: double/halve two-digit numbers by doubling/halving the tens first.
36 Pictures and words	● Choose and use appropriate operations and efficient calculation strategies (eg mental, mental with jottings) to solve problems.	● **Choose and use appropriate operations (including multiplication and division) to solve word problems.**	● **Choose and use appropriate number operations and appropriate ways of calculating (mental, mental with jottings, pencil and paper) to solve problems.**
37 Squares in squares	● Solve mathematical problems, recognise simple patterns, generalise and predict. Suggest extensions by asking *What if...?* or *What could I try next?*	● Solve mathematical problems or puzzles, recognise simple patterns and relationships, generalise and predict. Suggest extensions by asking *What if...?*	● Solve mathematical problems, recognise and explain patterns, generalise and predict. Suggest extensions by asking *What if...?*
38 How many ways?	● Solve mathematical problems, recognise simple patterns, generalise and predict. Suggest extensions by asking *What if...?* or *What could I try next?*	● Solve mathematical problems, recognise simple patterns, generalise and predict. Suggest extensions by asking *What if...?*	● Solve mathematical problems, recognise and explain patterns, generalise and predict. Suggest extensions by asking *What if...?*
39 Tower blocks	● Solve mathematical problems, recognise simple patterns, generalise and predict. Suggest extensions by asking *What if...?* or *What could I try next?*	● Solve mathematical problems, recognise simple patterns, generalise and predict. Suggest extensions by asking *What if...?*	● Solve mathematical problems, recognise and explain patterns, generalise and predict. Suggest extensions by asking *What if...?*

Title of lesson	Tracking back Year 2 objectives	Year 3 objectives	Tracking forwards Year 4 objectives
40 Building blocks	● Solve mathematical problems, recognise simple patterns, generalise and predict. Suggest extensions by asking *What if...?* or *What could I try next?*	● Solve mathematical problems, recognise simple patterns, generalise and predict. Suggest extensions by asking *What if...?*	● Solve mathematical problems, recognise and explain patterns, generalise and predict. Suggest extensions by asking *What if...?*
41 Up and away	● Explain how a problem was solved orally and, where appropriate, in writing.	● Explain methods and reasoning orally and where appropriate, in writing.	● Explain methods and reasoning about numbers orally and in writing.
42 Mix and match	● Use mental addition and subtraction, simple multiplication and division, to solve simple word problems involving numbers in real life', money or measures, using one or two steps. ● Explain how a problem was solved.	● Solve word problems involving numbers in 'real life', money and measures, using one or more steps, including finding totals and giving change, and working out which coins to pay. Explain how the problem was solved.	● Use all four operations to solve word problems involving numbers in 'real life', money and measures (including time).
43 How old?	● Use mental addition and subtraction, simple multiplication and division, to solve simple word problems involving numbers in real life', money or measures, using one or two steps. ● Explain how a problem was solved.	● Solve word problems involving numbers in 'real life', money and measures, using one or more steps.	● Use all four operations to solve word problems involving numbers in 'real life', money and measures (including time).
44 Big spender	● Use mental addition and subtraction, simple multiplication and division, to solve simple word problems involving numbers in real life', money or measures, using one or two steps. ● Explain how a problem was solved.	● Solve word problems involving numbers in 'real life', money and measures, using one or more steps.	● Use all four operations to solve word problems involving numbers in 'real life', money and measures (including time).
45 How much?	● Recognise all coins and begin to use £.p notation for money (for example, know that £4.65 indicates £4 and 65p). ● Find totals, give change, and work out which coins to pay.	● Recognise all coins and notes. **Understand and use £.p notation** (for example, know that £3.06 is £3 and 6p).	● Divide a whole number of pounds by 2, 4, 5 or 10 to give £.p. ● Round up or down after division, depending on the context.
46 What's on?	● Solve a given problem by sorting, classifying and organising information in simple ways.	● **Solve a given problem by organising and interpreting numerical data in simple lists, tables and graphs.**	● Solve a problem by collecting, organising, representing and interpreting data in tables, charts and so on (including IT-generated).
47 Days and months	● Use and begin to read the vocabulary related to time. Use units of time and know the relationships between them (second, minute, hour, day, week).	● Use units of time and know the relationships between them (second, minute, hour, day, week, month, year).	● Use, read and write the vocabulary related to time.
48 Shape jigsaws	● Make/describe shapes, pictures and patterns using, solid shapes, templates, pinboard and elastic bands, squared paper, a programmable robot, and so on.	● Make and describe shapes and patterns: for example, explore the different shapes that can be made from four cubes. ● Relate solid shapes to pictures of them.	● Visualise 3D shapes from 2D drawings and identify simple nets of solid shapes.
49 Mirror, mirror...	● Begin to recognise line symmetry.	● Identify and sketch lines of symmetry in simple shapes, and recognise shapes with no lines of symmetry.	● Make shapes: for example, construct polygons by paper folding, and discuss properties such as lines of symmetry.
50 Angle-eater	● Recognise whole, half and quarter turns, to the left or right, clockwise or anti-clockwise. ● Know that a right angle is a measure of a quarter turn. Recognise right angles in squares and rectangles.	● Identify right angles in 2D shapes and the environment.	● Begin to know that a quarter turn is 90° or one right angle; half a right angle is 45°.

Mental maths starters

1 100 up, 100 down

Learning objective
(Y2) Count on or back in tens from any number up to 100.

You will need
Number stick (empty rod of approximately 1m with graduations for every tenth of the length).

What to do
● Start by holding the number stick in the centre with one hand. Place the other hand at the left end of the stick and tell the group that the count starts at zero and increases in tens up to 100 (on the right end).
● Count forwards and backwards in sequential order.
● Select numbers 'at random' to identify if the children have a positional sense of where multiples lie. Discuss strategies – for example, for 70, a child might count on from 50 or back from 100.

Target questions
● How many tens are in 60?
● How did you work it out so quickly? (During 'random' selection.)

2 Count up, count down

Learning objective
(Y2) Count on or back in ones from any number up to 100.

You will need
Number stick (empty rod of approximately 1m with graduations for every tenth of the length).

What to do
● Start by holding the stick in the centre with one hand. Place the other hand at the left end of the stick and tell the group that the count starts at 15 and increases in ones up to 25 (on the right end).
● Count forwards and backwards in sequential order.
● Select numbers 'at random' to identify if the children have a positional sense of where multiples lie. Discuss strategies – for example, for 23 a child might count on from the central point (20) or back two from the right (25).

Target questions
● What number is two more than ...?
● How did you work it out so quickly? (During 'random' selection.)

3 Odds and evens

Learning objective
(Y2) Recognise odd and even numbers.

You will need
Number stick (empty rod of approximately 1m with graduations for every tenth of the length).

What to do
● Start by holding the stick at the centre with one hand. Place the other hand at the left end and tell the group that the count starts at zero and increases in twos up to 20 (on the right end).
● Count forwards and backwards in sequential order.
● Select numbers 'at random' to identify if the children have a positional sense of where multiples lie. Discuss strategies – for example, for an answer of 12, a child might count on one space from the central point (10).

Target questions
● What do we call these numbers? (Even.)
● How did you work it out so quickly? (During 'random' selection.)

Learning objective
(Y2) Count on in steps of five to at least 30, from 0 or a small number.

You will need
Number stick (empty rod of approximately 1m with graduations for every tenth of the length).

4 Fives
What to do
● Start by holding the stick at the centre with one hand. Place the other hand at the left end of the stick and tell the group that the count starts at zero and increases in fives up to 50 (on the right end).
● Count forwards and backwards in sequential order.
● Select numbers 'at random' to see if the children have a positional sense of where multiples lie. Discuss strategies, such as couting back two fives from the end point (50), for an answer of 40.

Target questions
● What do all the numbers end in? (0 or 5.)
● How did you work your answer out so quickly? (During 'random' selection.)

Learning objective
(Y2) Say the number names to at least 100.

You will need
Number grid or number line (0–50); markers to record progress.

5 Say my number
What to do
● Tell the group that you are thinking of a number (0–50) for them to guess. They can only answer 'higher' or 'lower' to any suggestion.
● As guesses are taken, continually refine the search, using markers on the number grid or line to give the lowest and highest extremes within which the answer must fall.
● Encourage the children to give full sentences using increasingly precise mathematical language.

Target questions
● Can you find a good strategy for getting the answer quickly? (Such as roughly splitting the range in half each time).
● What would be a 'better' word than bigger?

Learning objective
(Y2) Say the number names to at least 100.

You will need
Number grid or number line (0 -50); markers to record progress.

6 Guess my number
What to do
● Tell the group that you are thinking of a number for them to guess. They can only answer 'higher' or 'lower' to any suggestion.
● Tell them that they can ask questions of a mathematical nature, such as: *Is it an even number?*; *Is it in the five-times table?*; *Does it end in 4?*; *Is it more than 30?*
● As guesses are taken, continually refine the search, by striking out or highlighting numbers from the grid or number line.
● Encourage the children to give full sentences using increasingly precise mathematical language.

Target questions
● If the answer is in the five-times table, what must the number end in?
● Why was that a good question? (For example, it may neatly sub-divide a large set of possible numbers.)

Learning objective
(Y2) Say the number names to at least 100.

You will need
Number fans (one per child).

7 What's my number?

What to do
● Tell the group that you are thinking of a number for them to guess. Explain that they must each choose a number and show it to you on a number fan.
● Ask individuals to tell you what their number is and how many tens/units that number has.
● Tell the child who has chosen the number closest to yours that your number is more or less in comparison. Recap for all the children to hear. For example: *44 is the nearest number to mine and it is more than my number.*
● Ask the children to guess again (based on this information) and continue the process until a solution is found.

Target questions
● Why did you choose that number?
● What is the lowest possible number?

Learning objective
(Y2) Say the number names to at least 100.

You will need
0–100 number line; individual whiteboards; removable memo labels.

8 Lots of numbers

What to do
● Provide three single digit numerals, asking the group to write a two-digit number from one or two of these (for example, aligning the digits three and seven to form 37).
● 'Record' suggestions on the number line by covering such numbers with removable memo labels.
● Compare the numbers that are suggested and try to find all the possible answers.

Target questions
● Can you find a larger number than this?
● How many tens does this number have?

Learning objective
(Y2) Read and write whole numbers to at least 100 in figures and words.

You will need
Individual whiteboards and pens.

9 Guess my word

What to do
● Ask each child to write *as a word* any number from 1 to 10 after you have given them a simple clue to narrow the range (such as: *my number is greater than 5.*)
● Look at the responses, using this to refine spelling as required.
● Choose children who have written and chosen words correctly to have turns acting as the teacher (as above).

Target questions
● Which numbers do we find hard to spell?
● Can we spell some numbers greater than 10?

Learning objective
(Y2) Know by heart: all
addition and subtraction
facts for each number to
at least 10.

You will need
Individual whiteboards and
pens.

10 Guess my sum

What to do
● Write an addition number sentence with a total of ten and conceal it from the group.
● Ask each child to write a number sentence for addition where the answer is ten. If you wish, offer a simple clue to narrow the range of possibilities, such as: *my two numbers are both odd numbers.*
● Look at the children's responses, using this to check for accurate recording and reliable calculation.
● A sentence matching your own can be rewarded with that child acting as the teacher (as above).

Target questions
● How is your sentence different to mine? (For example, 7 + 3 = 10 and 3 + 7 = 10.)
● How did you know the answer was ten?

Learning objective
(Y2) Know by heart all
addition and subtraction
facts for each number to
at least 10.

You will need
Large number strip featuring
a 0-10 number line
(unmarked except for the
appropriately located digits
1, 4, 5 and 8).

11 Make it up

What to do
● Show the children the 'ruler', explaining that it begins at zero and ends at ten. Say that some of the numbers are 'missing'.
● Ask for help in finding different distances (for example, as there is no marker for 3, we could 'measure' from 1 to 4 or from 5 to 8).
● Through trial and error, establish that all unit lengths from one to ten can be found.

Target questions
● How did you work this out? (Counting on, counting back, recall.)
● Can we do the same with four different starting numbers? (Through trial and improvement it is possible to find other suitable combinations that work equally well.)

Learning objective
(Y2) Know by heart all
addition and subtraction
facts for each number to
at least 10.

You will need
A large square of card
featuring the numbers 1, 2,
4 and 8 (randomly
scattered).

12 Combinations

What to do
● Practise simple number bonds sampling any two available numbers (such as 8 + 4 makes 12).
● Choose any number (maximum 15) and ask for this to be created using some or all of the numbers in combination (the numbers given allow for any whole number to be created within the given range).
● Discuss strategies such as starting with the largest permitted number.

Target questions
● How did you work it out?
● Are there any numbers which cannot be made?

Learning objective
(Y2) Recall addition and subtraction facts for each number up to 20.

You will need
A large square of card featuring the numbers 17, 3, 6 and 5 (randomly scattered).

13 More combinations

What to do

● Prepare some 'target' numbers under addition and/or subtraction. For example, 18 can be 'hit' with (17 + 6) – 5. Direct questions appropriate to individual needs.
● Discuss the strategies used (in the above example a number 'close to 18' is used initially).

Target questions

● How did you work it out?
● Can you make a number sentence up of your own?

Learning objectives
(Y2) Know by heart all addition and subtraction facts for each number up to 10.
(Y2) Recall doubles to 10 + 10.

You will need
A large leaf featuring a scattering of 10 big-eyed bugs; a second leaf to obscure some or all of the bugs.

14 Bugs

What to do

● Count the bugs on the leaf.
● Obscure some of the bugs and ask how many bugs are visible/hidden.

Target questions

● How many bugs would we need to hide to leave just four of them?
● How many eyes can you see? (Extends range of answers to 20.)

Learning objective
(Y2) Recall pairs of multiples of 10 that make 100.

You will need
Flashcards featuring multiples of 10 from 0-100 (zero is a multiple of 10). The complement is written on the reverse to give a total of 100.

15 Partners

What to do

● Present the cards in order, chanting to 100 and back to zero again.
● Shuffle the pack and present the cards one at a time. Each time, read the number and calculate the complement together. Reverse the card to confirm correct answers.

Target questions

● How did you work that out?
● How many tens in this number? How many more tens do we need to make 100?

Learning objective
(Y2) Count on or back in tens from any number up to 100.

You will need
A large calculator (projected version if available) or suitable counting software.

16 Calculator patterns

What to do
● Enter a starting number followed by a step operation (such as 56 + 10 =). With a basic calculator, repeated presses of the = key should generate a continuing sequence.
● Encourage prediction before checking.
● Repeat for subtraction.

Target questions
● What number will come next?
● What will be next if we go over 100?

Learning objective
(Y2) Add/subtract 9, 19, 11, 21.

You will need
A large calculator (projected version if available) or suitable counting software.

17 Calculator patterns (2)

What to do
● Enter a starting number followed by a step operation (such as 56 + 9 =). With a basic calculator, repeated presses of the = key should generate a continuing sequence.
● Encourage prediction before checking.
● Repeat for subtraction.
● Explore further sequences such as adding 19, 11 and 21.

Target questions
● What number will come next?
● What will be next if we go over 100?

Learning objective
(Y2) Recognise odd and even numbers.

You will need
A set of number cards to 20.

18 Even sort

What to do
● Ask the children to help you sort the cards into sets of odd and even numbers.
● For each subset, look at the common unit digits and group them (for example, 2 and 12; 6 and 16).
● Illustrate how only even numbers feature 0, 2, 4, 6 and 8 as unit digits.

Target questions
● Would a large number like 99 be even or odd?
● Can you tell me a huge odd number?

Learning objective
(Y2) Recognise odd and even numbers.

19 That's odd!

What to do

● Give each child a random number tile.
● Ask the children to hold hands with someone who is 'two more or less than them'. Two sequences should result (one odd, one even).
● Repeat with tiles re-distributed in a different order.

Target questions

● What do we call this sequence?
● What number would come next in the sequence here?

You will need
Number tiles starting from 1 (sufficient for each group member).

20 Two-times table

Learning objective
(Y2) Recall two-times table facts.

What to do

● Shuffle the cards and ask individuals to read the number sentence and calculate the answer.
● Target questions to the capabilities of individuals.
● Conduct the activity in reverse, showing the product and requesting the associated number sentence.

Target questions

● How did you know the answer? (Recall, doubling, counting in twos from zero, using known facts to derive those not known).
● What do you notice if we halve the answer?

You will need
Flash cards featuring number sentences for x2 facts on one side (such as 7 x 2 =) with the answer on the reverse.

21 Five-times table

Learning objective
(Y2) Recall five-times table facts.

What to do

● Shuffle the cards and ask individuals to read the number sentence and calculate the answer.
● Target questions to the capabilities of individuals
● Conduct the activity in reverse, showing the product and requesting the associated number sentence.

Target questions

● How did you know the answer? (Recall, counting in fives from zero, using known facts to derive those not known.)
● What do you notice about the unit digits?

You will need
Flash cards featuring number sentences for x5 facts on one side (such as 8 x 5 =) with the answer on the reverse.

22 Ten-times table

Learning objective
(Y2) Recall ten-times table and derive division facts.

You will need
Flash cards featuring number sentences for x10 facts on one side (such as 6 x 10 =) with the answer on the reverse.

What to do
● Shuffle the cards and ask individuals to read the number sentence and calculate the answer.
● Target questions to the capabilities of individuals.
● Conduct the activity in reverse, showing the product and requesting the associated number sentence.

Target questions
● How would we get back from 60 to 6?
● What do you notice about the unit digits?

23 Halves and doubles

Learning objective
(Y2) Derive doubles to 15 + 15 and corresponding halves.

You will need
Prepared square flash cards – each one featuring an even number (up to 20 or 30) on one side, with a horizontal fold through the mid-point. Folding the upper half forward and over should conceal that number and reveal a number which has half that value.

What to do
● Present a number and tell the children that it is a double. Ask for the number which has half its value.
● Reverse the above operation (doubling) if halving proves problematic.

Target questions
● What would we have to do to our answer to get back to our starting number?
● How did you know the answer?

24 Number families

Learning objective
(Y2) State a subtraction fact corresponding to an addition fact and vice versa.

You will need
Prepared card triangles (with a number in each corner to show an addition/subtraction 'family' such as 5, 3 and 8).

What to do
● Hold up a triangle, obscuring the total of two numbers with your grip. Ask for the total.
● Show all the numbers and ask the children for related (subtraction) number sentences.

Target questions
● Have we found all the possible number sentences for these numbers?
● Can we reverse these numbers in our number sentence? (Addition is commutative, subtraction is not.)

25 Number families (2)

What to do
● Hold up a triangle, obscuring the total with your grip. Ask for the product.
● Show all the numbers and ask for related (division/sharing) number sentences.

Target questions
● Have we found all the possible number sentences for these numbers?
● Can we reverse these numbers in our number sentence? (Multiplication is commutative, division is not.)

Learning objective
(Y2) Recall multiplication facts of the two-times table and deduce division facts.

You will need
Prepared card triangles (featuring a number in each corner to show a multiplication/division 'family' involving the two-times table such as 7, 2 and 14).

---

26 Make that 10

What to do
● Show the children a number tile. Ask them to provide the complementary number to make ten (such as four and six).
● Develop recall and/or strategies such as counting on.

Target questions
● How did you know the answer?
● How many more do you need?

Learning objective
(Y2) Recall all pairs with a total of 10.

You will need
Number tiles featuring single digits.

---

27 Make it 20

What to do
● Show a number tile. Ask for the complementary number for a total of 20 (such as 17 and 3).
● Develop recall and/or strategies such as counting on. Provide the top two rows of a 100-square to encourage counting on to ten (for single digit numbers), using this as a bridge for a further ten.

Target questions
● How did you know the answer?
● How many more do you need?

Learning objective
(Y2) Recall all pairs with a total of 20.

You will need
Number tiles featuring numbers (maximum of 20); a 100-square.

<table>
<tr><td>**Learning objective**
(Y2) Know by heart all addition and subtraction facts for each number up to 10.</td></tr>
</table>

Learning objective
(Y2) Know by heart all addition and subtraction facts for each number up to 10.

You will need
Tin; real coins (1p, 2p).

28 Money box

What to do
● Say that you have been to the shops with 10p and have bought something. Ask the children to close their eyes and listen to the change (1p coins only) being dropped in the tin.
● Ask: *How much did I spend therefore?*
● Repeat the activity, this time using change from 20p using 1p and/or 2p coins.

Target questions
● How many twos make 20p?
● How did you work it out?

Learning objective
(Y2) Say the number names to at least 100.

You will need
Individual whiteboards; a large standard dice.

29 Top numbers

What to do
● Invite each child to sketch a small rectangle with three sub-divisions for entering a hundreds, a tens and a units digit.

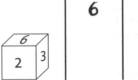

H	T	U
	6	

● Roll the dice three times, after each throw individuals decide whether to commit this to the hundred, tens or units column. The aim is to secure the highest possible number. These values must be read aloud as a number.
● After the game discuss the value of individuals' digits.

Target questions
● How much is that digit worth?
● Using the same digits, what would be the smallest possible number?

Learning objective
(Y2) Recognise multiples of 5. Recall multiplication facts in the five-times table.
(Y2) Count on in steps of 5 to at least 30, from zero or a small number.

You will need
Several large card squares, some featuring '5', others '3'.

30 Make it up (2)

What to do
● Rehearse double and triple number bonds by asking questions requiring a total of 5s and/or 3s.
● Provide a target number in the range 8–20 and ask for that to be made from just fives and/or threes. (It is possible to make every whole number across the given range.)

Target questions
● *How did you work it out?* (Knowledge of multiplication facts, modifying an earlier combination …)
● *Can this total be made a different way?*

Learning objective
(Y2) Know by heart all addition and subtraction facts for each number up to at least 10.

You will need
Number cards 1-10.

31 Countdown

What to do

● Align the cards in numerical order, face up.
● Two players take turns to turn over either one, two or three numbers starting at 10 and heading downwards. The challenge is to be the person who gets to turn over the digit 1.
● A controlling (winning) strategy involves 'forcing' your opponent to turn over the number 4 (by ending your penultimate turn on 5).

Target questions

● What will three less give me here?
● Does anyone think they have a strategy?

Learning objective
(Y2) Partition a two-digit number into tens and ones.
(Y2) Read and write in words and figures, numbers to 100.

You will need
Flashcards featuring 20, 30, 40, 50, 1, 2, 3, 4 and 5 in words; place value cards.

32 What's my number? (1)

What to do

● Invite individuals to build a number and to read it aloud. For example, 20 and 4 make 24. Ask them to try to make that amount with the place value cards.
● Use the place value cards to reinforce the value of each digit.
● Look at spelling patterns within words.

Target questions

● How many tens are in this digit?
● How much is that digit worth?

Learning objectives
(Y2) Partition a two-digit number into tens and ones.
(Y2) Read and write in words and figures, numbers to100.

You will need
Flashcards featuring 60, 70, 80, 90, 6, 7, 8 and 9 in words; place value cards.

33 What's my number? (2)

What to do

● Invite individuals to build a number and to read it aloud (as above). Ask them to try to make that amount with the place value cards.
● Use the place value cards to reinforce the value of each digit.
● Look at spelling patterns within words.

Target questions

● How many tens are in this digit?
● How much is that digit worth?

Learning objective
(Y2) Partition a two-digit number into tens and ones.

You will need
Demonstration place value cards; individual whiteboards.

34 What's my number? (3)

What to do

- Use the large place value cards to create a two-digit number.
- Ask each child to make a picture on their whiteboard of what they will see when you 'disassemble' the digit cards.
- Extend to three-digit numbers if appropriate. Focus on the value of each digit.

Target questions

- How much is this digit worth?
- If we have a number like this (22), how many times more is this digit worth (tens) than this digit (units)?

Learning objectives
(Y2) Recognise odd and even numbers.
(Y2) Derive near doubles.

You will need
A line of number cards in ascending order from 0–10.

35 Next door

What to do

- Ask individuals to pick any pair of numbers which appear 'next door' to one another (consecutively) on the number line.
- Hold these up and ask for the total. Record the answer and return the cards to their places.
- Continue with other pairings, drawing attention to the 'near double' property of such combinations.

Target questions

- Are your answers odd or even?
- Will they always be odd?
- How did you use doubling to help you? (Double the larger and subtract one, double the smaller and add one.)

Learning objective
(Y2) Derive doubles of multiples of 5, halves of multiples of 10.

You will need
Prepared square flash cards – each one features a multiple of 10 (up to 100) on one side with a horizontal fold through the mid point. Folding the upper half forward and over should conceal that number and reveal a number which has half that value.

36 Halve it

What to do

- Present a number and tell the children that it is a multiple of ten. Ask them to tell you the number which has half its value.
- Reverse the above operation (doubling) if halving proves problematic.

Target questions

- What would we have to do to our answer to get back to our starting number?
- How did you know the answer?

Learning objective
(Y2) Derive doubles to 15 + 15 and corresponding halves.

You will need
Two sets of place value cards (10, 1, 2, 3, 4 and 5.

37 Double it

What to do

- Ask volunteers to make a two-digit number from the selection provided (such as 12).
- Explain that to make a double you are going to ask someone else to select the same two cards.
- Demonstrate how the numbers can be combined by partitioning them both and regrouping the tens and units separately (for example 10 + 10 and 2 + 2).
- Record this process and establish the total.

Target questions

- Are our doubles even or odd?
- Why does this happen?

Learning objective
(Y2) Derive doubles of multiples of 5, halves of multiples of 10.

You will need
Two sets of place value cards (10, 20, 30, 40 and 5).

38 More doubles

What to do

- Ask a volunteer to make a multiple of five with the available cards.
- Explain that to make a double you are going to ask someone else to select the same cards.
- Record the process of partioning tens and units, then recounting, and establish the total.

Target questions

- If our double is 70, what operation would we need to do to get us back to 35?
- What do all our doubles end in?

Learning objective
(Y2) Recall pairs of multiples of 10 that make 100.
(Y2) Count on or back in tens from any number up to 100.

You will need
A tin; real coins (5p, 10p).

39 Money box (2)

What to do

- Explain that you have been to the shops with £1 and have bought something. Ask the children to close their eyes and listen to the change (10p coins only) being dropped in the tin.
- Ask: *How much did I spend therefore?*
- Do the same with change from £1 using 5p coins.

Target questions

- How did you work it out?
- How many 5p coins make £1?

Learning objective
(Y2) Know by heart all addition and subtraction facts for each number up to 10.

You will need
A large whiteboard.

40 Money puzzle

What to do
- Pose some word problems. For example, explain that two people have 10p altogether, and that one person has 2p more than the other.
- Invite the children to work out some possible amounts for each person.
- Look at all the combinations to see which one gives the correct difference.

Target questions
- Have we found all the ways of making 10p?
- Which answer gives a difference of two?

Learning objective
(Y2) State the subtraction corresponding to a given addition fact and vice versa.

You will need
Prepared card triangles (featuring a number in each corner to show an addition/subtraction 'family' such as 7, 13 and 20).

41 Number families (3)

What to do
- Hold up a triangle, obscuring the total with your grip. Ask for the total.
- Show all the numbers and ask for related (subtraction) number sentences.

Target questions
- Have we found all the possible number sentences for these numbers?
- Can we reverse these numbers in our number sentence? (Addition is commutative, subtraction is not.)

Learning Objective
(Y3) Recognise multiples of 5. Recall multiplication facts in five-times table.

You will need
Prepared card triangles (featuring a number in each corner to show a multiplication/division 'family' involving the five-times table, such as 7, 5 and 35).

42 Number families (4)

What to do
- Hold up a triangle, obscuring the total with your grip. Ask for the product.
- Show all the numbers and ask for related (division/sharing) number sentences.

Target questions
- Have we found all the possible number sentences for these numbers?
- Can we reverse these numbers in our number sentence? (Multiplication is commutative, division is not.)

43 Calculator patterns (3)

What to do
● Enter zero in your calculator as the start number followed by a step operation (such as 0 + 5 =). With a basic calculator, repeated presses of the = key should generate a continuing sequence.
● Encourage prediction before checking.
● Explore related sequences such as adding three or four.

Target questions
● What number will come next?
● What happens with the unit digits?

44 Calculator patterns (4)

What to do
● Enter 2 in your calculator as the start number followed by a step operation (such as 2 + 5 =). With a basic calculator, repeated presses of the = key should generate a continuing sequence.
● Encourage prediction before checking.
● Explore related sequences such as adding 3 or 4, starting from any small number.

Target questions
● What number will come next?
● What happens with the units digits?

45 Find a partner (1)

What to do
● Supply a number tile to each individual starting from 1.
● Choose a target total (such as 6). Ask the children to find a partner to make this total.
● Select different target totals.

Target questions
● Does everyone have a partner?
● If 'no' to the above, why not?

Learning objective
(Y2) Know by heart all addition and subtraction facts for each number up to 10.

You will need
Number tiles 1–10.

46 Find a partner (2)

What to do
- Arrange the number tiles in ascending order.
- Choose a target total (such as nine). Ask the children to find all the pairs of cards giving this total.
- Select different target totals.

Target questions
- Does every number have a 'partner'?
- If 'no' to the above, why not?

Learning objective
(Y2) Count on in steps of 5 to at least 30, from 0 or a small number.
(Y2) Recall two-times table.

You will need
100-square; dry wipe markers (in two colours).

47 Crossover

What to do
- Count on in steps of 5, marking each 'station' on the 100-square (up to 30) with a dry wipe pen.
- Use the same 100-square and a differently-coloured pen to mark the 'stations' of the two-times table (up to 30 again).
- Look to see where the two-times and five-times tables 'overlap'.

Target questions
- What's special about these (double-coloured) numbers? (All multiples of 10.)
- What would be the next number to be coloured twice?

Learning objective
(Y2) Say the number names to at least 100.

You will need
Large number tiles (1 to 9); dry wipe marker; 100-square.

48 Number crunchers

What to do
- Select any three single-digit number tiles. Ask for suggestions of two-digit numbers that can be created from these.
- Record suggestions on a 100-square (circling the number with a dry wipe marker).
- Look for spatial patterns resulting from all possible combinations.

Target questions
- Have we found them all?
- How do we say this number?

Learning objective
(Y2) Recall two-times, five-times and ten-times table facts.

You will need
Flash cards featuring number sentences for two-times, five-times and ten-times facts on one side (such as 6 x 2 =) with the answer on the reverse.

49 Know your facts

What to do
● Shuffle the cards and ask individuals to read the number sentence and calculate the answer.
● Target questions to the capabilities of individuals.
● Conduct the activity in reverse, showing the product and requesting the associated number sentence.

Target questions
● How did you know the answer? (Recall, doubling, counting in twos from zero, using known facts to derive those not known.)
● What do you notice if we halve the answer?
● Do any of our number sentences share the same answer? (for example, 6 x 5 and 3 x 10).

Learning objective
(Y2) Recognise odd and even numbers.

You will need
Number cards 1 to 10.

50 What's the score?

What to do
● Shuffle the cards and place them face down. Establish two teams.
● The teams take turns to pick three cards. Even numbers are added, odd numbers are taken away. If the number falls below zero, the score for that round is zero. Shuffle after each turn.
● After a few turns, see who has scored the most 'points'.

Target questions
● Is this number odd or even?
● How many odd/even numbers are there in the set of cards?

Number cards

1	2	3
4	5	6
7	8	9
10	11	12

Count me in!

Learning Objectives
(Y2) Count reliably up to 100 objects by grouping them: for example, in tens, then in fives or twos.
(Y3) Count larger collections by grouping them: for example, in tens, then other numbers.

Mental Starter
See the starter activity, '100 up, 100 down' on page 10.

You will need
Collections of small cubes; money; buttons or counters; photocopiable page 29 (one per child).

Moving on
● Direct those children who count confidently and reliably in steps of 5 or 10 towards the fact that each sheet contains an upper and lower section with space for 25 objects. Can they count in steps of 25 up to (and beyond) 100?
● Ask the children to develop their own chart with rows of (say) three or four. Can they total collections of objects by counting in such steps?

Whole class work
● Ask the children to think about times when we might count in 'real-life' situations. Do we have to be accurate on these occasions or is it sometimes just to get an *idea* of the quantity?
● Hold up a jar of cubes or any collection containing about 50 objects. Invite estimates for the total number of objects and discuss whether these are reasonable.
● Engage the children in counting the objects out for you. Explain that you are going to remove two at a time to make things a little quicker. Check that they are comfortable counting in twos to the given total.

Group work
● Explain that the group are going to look at collections of things – using counting in different steps to find their totals.
● Start with a pile of money, shells or any other collection you have available. Demonstrate counting in ones to find the total number of objects (for example, 42). Double-check the total by engaging the children in a second count.
● Remove a few objects and repeat the exercise, counting in tens. After each ten, begin a new pile and use this base-ten grouping to tally the overall total.
● Explore counting two objects at a time, sliding them to a new position to avoid miscalculation. Then count back from the total for confirmation.

Individual work
● Ask the children to count the circles shown on page 29. Talk to them about rows, columns and the overall array, explaining that this will help them to record and total the collections they will be making.
● Engage the children in taking turns to grab, with one hand only, the maximum number of cubes (or similar) possible. Ask them to place each of their objects on a circle on the activity sheet, systematically filling up sections as they go.
● Use this as an opportunity to count the objects in tens and/or fives. Build on to these collections with further rounds, using a second copy of the sheet if appropriate.

Plenary
● Invite the children to colour in the number of circles that their cubes occupied. Use the results as a basis for comparison. Ask why some children can grab more than others, considering how the area of the hand may have some impact on the outcomes.

Potential difficulties	Further support
Miscounting due to an unstable recall of the sequence of numbers.	Refer back to a visual representation such as a 100-grid.
Randomly filling available circles – the child has not recognised the intention of counting by grouping.	Refer back to practical benefits such as counting pairs of children. Use a number line as a prompt for counting in regular steps other than 1.

Name _____

Count me in!

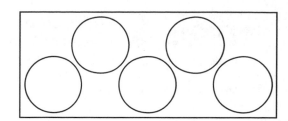

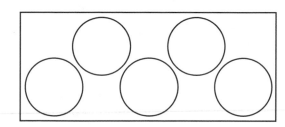

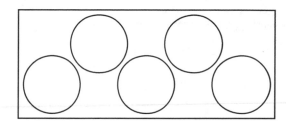

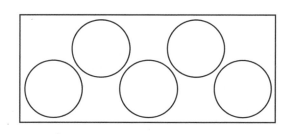

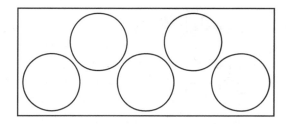

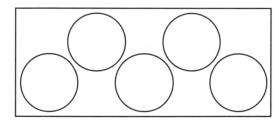

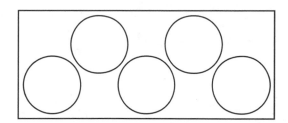

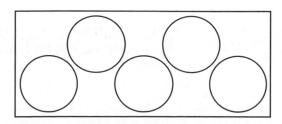

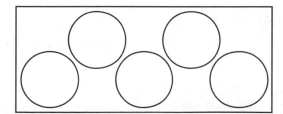

Takes and adders!

Learning objectives
(Y2) Count on or back in ones or tens, starting from any two-digit number.
(Y3) Count on or back in tens or hundreds, starting from any two- or three-digit number.
(Y4) Recognise and extend number sequences formed by counting from any number in steps of constant size, extending beyond zero when counting back: for example, count on in steps of 25 to 500, and then back to, say, 100.

Mental Starter
See the starter activity, 'Count up, count down' on page 10.

You will need
Photocopiable page 31 (one per child); three standard dice; a simple calculator (confirm that the calculator can add constantly by entering 10 + 10 followed by repeated presses of the = key); 100 square (Whole class work only).

Moving on
● Roll three dice as before, but 'give' each child an additional 100 to create a relatively low three-digit number. Use this to repeatedly subtract ten (for example, 113 – 10 = = = =).
● Use three numeral dice and push them together to form a three-digit starting number. Proceed as earlier, this time adding/subtracting 10 or 100 each time.

Whole class work
● Focus on a large 100 square, explaining that you want to look at counting in tens from a small number. Begin by picking a number in the upper half of the grid. Ask the class how the grid can help find a number which is *10 more*. Repeat with other numbers to establish the fact that a vertical drop of one space represents 10 more.
● Select a number from the top row of the grid and invite individuals to say the sequence all the way down that column. Alternatively you could chant with the whole class in unison.
● When the final number is given for the sequence, ask what number would come next if the grid were to be extended. Then, select other numbers from the top line of the grid, proceeding as above.

Group work
● Look at a 100 square and, starting from any number in the top row, count on 10 each time by scanning down the appropriate column. Ask: *What do you notice about this column of numbers?*

Individual work
● This game will use a calculator to check the ability to add or subtract a number repeatedly to make a sequence. The sequence is recorded along the body of the snake. Remove the 100 square as a visual prompt.
● Ask each child to roll and total three dice in order to give a unique start number. If a total has already been created by another child, throw again to generate a different number.
● Demonstrate how to use the calculator for adding 10 to their start number, taking care not to cancel the display afterwards. Record this on a snake and encourage the children to predict what a further 10 would make. Test predictions by pressing the = key.
● Allow the children to proceed using mental calculation first, recording on the sheet and checking each step. The nine available spaces on each snake should allow the children to reach a number around 100. Add on a further one or two steps to ascertain whether they are secure with numbers crossing into the hundreds.

Plenary
● Collect the recorded work and refer to one snake from each sheet. Ask the appropriate child a question for them to answer blindly (with further prompts if necessary). For example: *I see one of your numbers is 34. What number came next on your sheet?* or: *What was your largest number less than 100?*

Potential difficulties	Further support
Some children may record incorrectly where one number sounds like another (such as 40 for 14).	Ensure that words are clearly audible and focus on word formation.
Crossing the boundary of 10/100 can be difficult in ascending or descending number sequences.	Refer back to the 100 square and consider extending with an extra couple of rows.

Takes and adders!

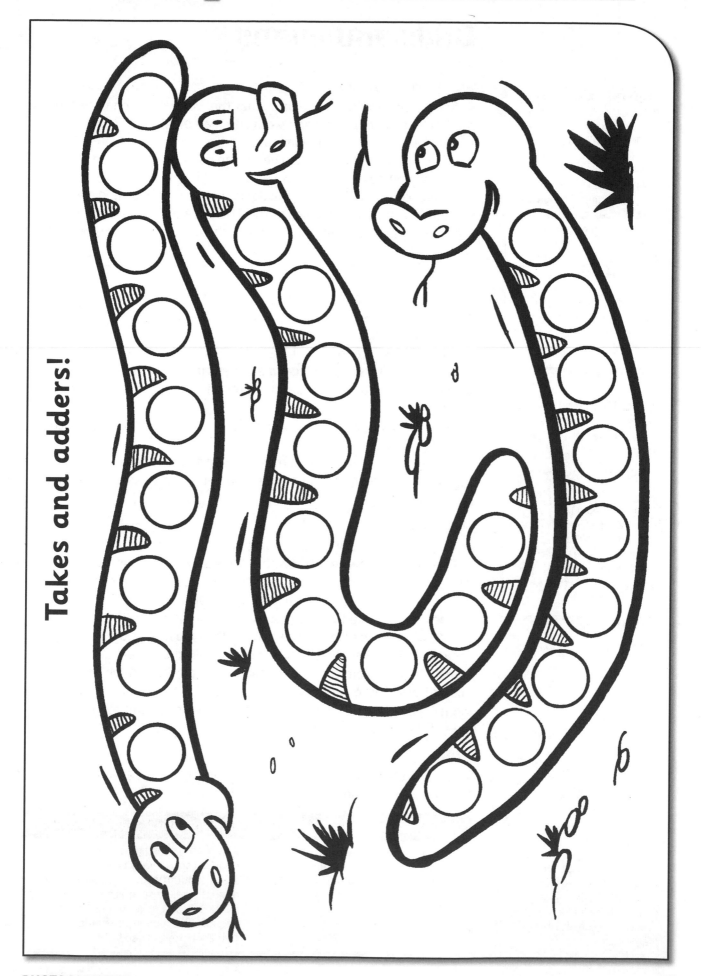

Odds and evens

Learning Objectives
(Y2) Count on in twos from and back to zero or any small number, and recognise odd and even numbers to at least 30.
(Y3) Count on or back in twos starting from any two-digit number, and recognise odd and even numbers to at least 100.
(Y4) Recognise odd and even numbers up to 1000, and some of their properties, including the outcome of sums or differences of pairs of odd/even numbers.

Mental Starter
See the starter activity, 'Odds and evens' on page 10.

You will need
Cubes or 2p coins; a number line; set of 1–20 or 1–50 number cards per pair; photocopiable page 00 (per pair); 100 square (Whole class section only).

Whole class work
- Ask the children to think about what the word 'odd' means. Encourage them to think about its meaning outside mathematics as well as the specific use of the word in numeracy.
- Invite individual children to give you an odd number, asking them to explain why they believe this is so.
- Reference to a 100 square will demonstrate that odds and evens are evident in alternating columns of the 100 square. Talk about the final digits in any given column, as this gives the odd/even identity of such sequences.

Group work
- Practise counting in twos using 2p coins or paired blocks of interlocking cubes. Extend beyond 10 or 20 to emphasise the repetition of the unit digits.
- Show the generation of this sequence as a movement along a number line, stressing the idea of a generating rule ('plus 2' each time). Check that the group associate this sequence with the idea of even numbers.
- Talk about the concept of even numbers in familiar contexts (such as queuing in pairs).
- Repeat the activity, this time developing an appreciation of odd numbers (talk about the generating rule being the same as for even numbers).

Paired work
- Provide each pair with page 33 and a set of numeral cards.
- Demonstrate how to play. Shuffle the numeral cards and lay them face down. One person needs to fill the left side of the sheet with odd numbers and the other must fill the right side with even numbers.
- The children take turns to pick a card from the top of the pack. They decide whether they may claim it. If so, they must copy the numeral on their side of the sheet. Talk through how they know their claim is correct. Where a card cannot be claimed, it is placed face up on a 'discard' pile. This pile can be reshuffled if all the original cards have been used before any one player has had the opportunity to fill their side of the sheet.

Plenary
- Explore three-digit numbers to identify whether individuals are ready to generalise for odd and even properties.

Moving on
- Ask each child to rearrange their odd or even cards in ascending order.
- Identify how well this is achieved and question whether 'missing' odd/even numbers can be identified to complete a consecutive sequence.

Potential difficulties	Further support
Some children may have the misconception that a two-digit number with an odd tens digit is automatically an odd number.	Reference to the appropriate column of a 100 square may help. If significant difficulties persist, restrict cards to several sets in the range 1–10. A tower of multilink can be broken into two to see whether two equal towers can be created.

Odds and evens

Step by step

Mental Starter
See the starter activity, 'Fives' on page 11.

You will need
Photocopiable page 35 (one per child); interlocking cubes (ideally, 20mm sided). Large number line and marker (Whole class section only).

Whole class work

● Ask the class to think of a multiple of 3 between, say, 10 and 20. Locate and mark this on a large number line. Ask first for the next multiple of 3, followed by the one before. Show both of these numbers by counting on and back three units from the initial number.

● Repeat the above process, this time beginning with a multiple of 4 between 10 and 20.

● You might explain that it is sometimes useful to find a multiple of a number by working forwards or backwards from a known fact. For example, to find the multiple 3 times 9, you can first recall that 3 times 10 is 30 and then work backwards.

Group work

● Generate the 3, 4 or 5 sequence by drawing a pattern of triangles, squares or pentagons and noting the number of lines required to create them. For example: one square – four lines; two squares – eight lines … .

● Encourage the children to predict – ask: *How many lines will I need to draw for ten squares?*

● Link this work to the group's emerging capabilities with regard to one or more of these sequences.

Individual work

● Select whether to focus on steps of 3, 4 or 5 (you may vary this according to the individual child's needs).

● Starting from zero and using the grid on page 35, place a cube on the number 3 (or 4 or 5). Record the number in one of the snakes.

● Place a differently-coloured cube, a further step of three/four/five on the grid.

● Continue in this way, each time recording the 'staging posts' in the snake. Encourage the children to predict forthcoming stopping points. When a sequence is completed, ask each child to clear their grid of any cubes, and to freshly mark out their recorded staging posts using ten cubes (or less where applicable). Ask: *Can you see a pattern? How does the pattern go?*

● Use the second snake to work with a different step size, starting as before from zero. Alternatively, consider extending the pattern to beyond 30, or exploring a *descending* sequence as detailed in 'moving on' (below left).

Moving on
● Begin to explore divisibility rules: the sum of the digits in any multiple of 3 is either 3 or a multiple thereof; multiples of 5 end in 0 or 5; multiples of 4 remain even after being halved.
● Look at counting on from (say) one or two.
● Engage in *counting back* in steps from 30 (or thereabouts).

Plenary

● Concentrate on looking for the patterns that the different step sizes made. Can the children cover the numbers on the snake and predict the next step(s)?

Potential difficulties	Further support
Children may be tempted to use counting on to bypass laying out blocks; they may do this incorrectly by including the staging post as the first item in that count.	Demonstrate the benefits of laying out blocks to remind us how to count the sequence of steps.

Step by step

1 one	2 two	3 three	4 four	5 five	6 six	7 seven	8 eight	9 nine	10 ten
11 eleven	12 twelve	13 thirteen	14 fourteen	15 fifteen	16 sixteen	17 seventeen	18 eighteen	19 nineteen	20 twenty
21 twenty-one	22 twenty-two	23 twenty-three	24 twenty-four	25 twenty-five	26 twenty-six	27 twenty-seven	28 twenty-eight	29 twenty-nine	30 thirty

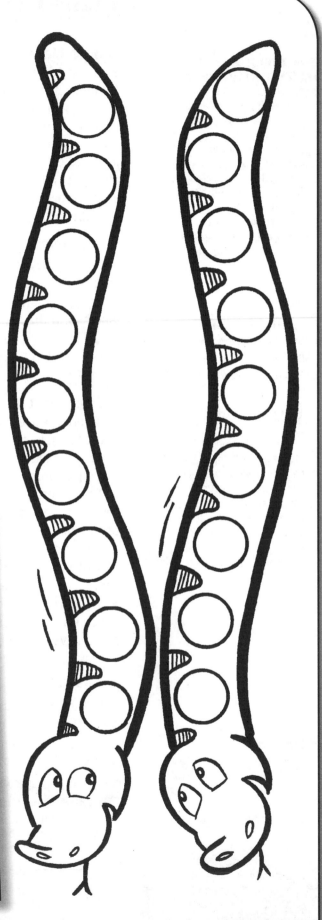

Cover up

Whole class work
- Use a 100 square and a marker to locate the children's suggestions for multiples of 5. After a while the positional significance will be clear; that is, only two columns will be sampled.
- Starting at 4, build the sequence of the multiples of 4. When 24 is reached it will be apparent that the spatial arrangement is not limited to just two columns as before. Ask the class to predict where the next multiple of 4 would be in the column headed by the 4, given that 4 and 24 have already been covered. Check this by counting on from 24.
- If time allows, explore the spatial arrangement for multiples of 3.

Group work
- Revise knowledge of 2-, 5- and 10-times tables using a suitable software application based on recall. Alternatively, use an empty counting stick (sub-divided to give ten sections) to attach self-adhesive labels with the appropriate stations pre-written on each one. Place these labels in sequential order starting from zero, or supply labels out of sequence to encourage positional awareness.

Paired work
- Explain that the purpose of the game is to help the children to remember those numbers in the 2, 5 and 10 times tables. Cut photocopiable page 37 in half to provide one board per child. If more than two children are involved, it is fine for them to have identical playing boards.
- The children take it in turns to throw the prepared dice. They may cover a square on their board with a counter if that number is a multiple of the dice outcome. To that end, remind the group of the features of the 2-times (even), 5-times (ends in 5 or 0) and 10-times tables (ends in 0). Note that only one number can be claimed each turn, even though some dice outcomes could offer a claim for two or more vacant squares.
- Try to create an opportunity for children to declare the 'table fact' which enables a square to be claimed. Assess how well facts are known, and analyse how others are being derived.
- Play continues until one child has covered all the numbers.

Plenary
- Return to the counting stick – this time without the use of sticky labels. For a given multiplication family, point to a position on the counting stick and encourage recall (or derivation from known facts by, for example, counting on/back or doubling/halving).

Potential difficulties	Further support
Numbers featuring an odd tens digit (such as 32) could be viewed incorrectly as being odd.	Try counting in twos to such totals or consider visual representations partitioned into equal halves.

Learning Objectives
(Y2) Know by heart facts for the 2 and 10 multiplication tables. Recognise two-digit multiples of 5.
(Y3) Know by heart facts for the 2, 5 and 10 multiplication tables. Recognise three-digit multiples of 50 and 100.
(Y4) Know by heart facts for the 2, 3, 4, 5 and 10 multiplication tables.

Mental Starter
See the starter activity, 'Say my number' on page 11.

You will need
Dice labelled 2, 2, 5, 5, 10, 10 (this will support 2–4 players); photocopiable page 37 (half a sheet per child); cubes or counters; a counting stick and self-adhesive labels or recall software; a marker; 100 square.

Moving on
- Modify the dice (replace one 10 and one 5 for two 4s) to allow for multiples of 4. If this proves too big a step, modify the board to include a narrower range of numbers (such as a maximum number 20).
- Extend the range to enable multiplication facts up to 50.

Cover up

30	28	☆	15
(cube)	9	12	(splat)
14	(splat)	20	35
24	8	22	☆
40	☆	10	18
(splat)	15	(cube)	25

Hundred up

Learning objectives
(Y2) Read and write whole numbers to at least 100 in figures and words.
(Y3) Read and write whole numbers to at least 1000 in figures and words.
(Y4) Read and write whole numbers to at least 10,000 in figures and words, and know what each digit represents.

Mental Starter
See the starter activity, 'Guess my number' on page 11.

You will need
Three numeral dice each labelled 1 to 6; enlarged version of the stimulus poster (photocopiable page 39); prepare a game board with '100+' to '600+' written within separate large rectangles or cells and copy it onto card for each child; self-adhesive labels; a large representation of a personal cheque as detailed in the Plenary (below).

Moving On
● Modify the dice, photocopiable poster and game board to enable arrangements in the 7, 8 and 9 hundreds.

Whole class work
● Write a 3 digit number such as 247 on the board and explain that you want to 'write a cheque' using words as well as figures. Ask individual children to say the whole number. Break each section of this into smaller components, noting the inclusion and spelling of words such as *hundred* and *and*.
● Try with a number such as 406 which introduces further complexity in terms of the place value. The written outcome is shorter in length.

Group work
● Roll three numeral dice to generate three numbers. Using these as digits, ask the children to create numbers by ordering them in different ways. Use the outcomes to demonstrate writing the numbers in words.
● Show the children the poster on photocopiable page 39 and talk about it together. It shows a mechanical 'number generator'. Explain that this poster will help them with the number spellings in their individual work. Draw their attention to spellings such as *fifty* instead of *fivety*; forty instead of *fourty* and so on.

Paired work
● Provide each child with the prepared game board (see 'You will need' opposite), self-adhesive labels and pens, and each pair with a set of three numeral dice. The purpose of the task is to help the children to write numbers in words. The aim of the game is to cover each of the six rectangles on the game board with appropriately written numbers.
● Each child takes a turn to roll all three dice. These are then arranged in any preferred order to make a number (minimum 111, maximum 666).
● They then record the number in words on their adhesive label (using the stimulus poster for support) and post it over the appropriate rectangle on the game board (for example, 236 can be placed over the 200+ square as it falls 'in the 200s').
● The use of numeral dice should make it relatively straightforward to explore different combinations from the dice outcomes. Some children may need to be reminded of this strategic element of the game. Play continues until all rectangles are covered (sometimes it will not be possible to cover a cell if the dice outcomes are unfavourable).
● Review the task by asking each child to read aloud their recorded numbers.

Plenary
● Return to the group work, this time using the idea of a personal cheque as a real-life application of writing numbers in words. If possible, create a giant cheque book to engage the children in forming numbers in words for a given figure (written numerically in pounds).

Potential difficulties	Further support
Some words can prove problematic, notable examples including fifty, forty and twelve.	In such cases, systematic and guided help through the stimulus poster may be required.

Hundred up

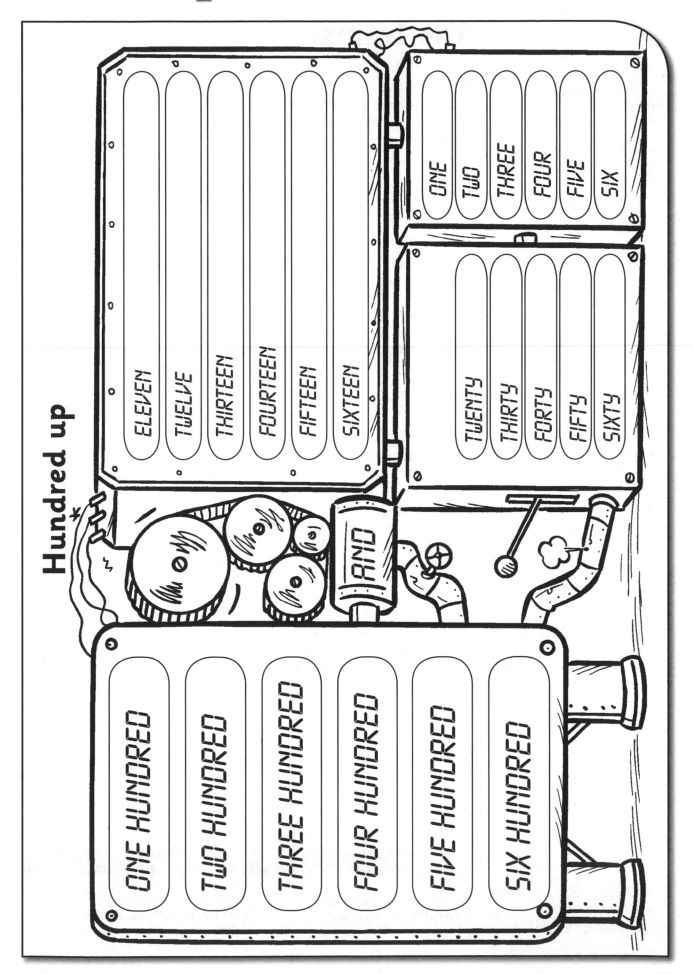

ELEVEN
TWELVE
THIRTEEN
FOURTEEN
FIFTEEN
SIXTEEN

ONE
TWO
THREE
FOUR
FIVE
SIX

TWENTY
THIRTY
FORTY
FIFTY
SIXTY

AND

ONE HUNDRED
TWO HUNDRED
THREE HUNDRED
FOUR HUNDRED
FIVE HUNDRED
SIX HUNDRED

Top totals

Learning Objectives
(Y2) Know what each digit in a two-digit number represents, including 0 as a place holder, and partition two-digit numbers into a multiple of ten and ones (TU).
(Y3) Know what each digit represents in numbers up to 1000, and partition three-digit numbers into a multiple of 100, a multiple of ten and ones (HTU).
(Y4) Multiply or divide any integer up to 1000 by 10 (whole-number answers), and understand the effect.

Mental Starter
See the starter activity, 'What's my number?' on page 12.

You will need
Two dice per pair (faces labelled blank, 10, 20, 30, 40, 50 and; blank 1, 2, 3, 4, 5); photocopiable page 41 (one set of cards per child); demonstration place value cards (optional).

Moving On
● Modify the tens dice with larger multiples of ten (for example 60, 70) and create a 100 place value card to cope with some of the larger totals.

Whole class work
● Write a three-digit number on the board and invite an individual to create that number using a demonstration set of place value cards. When the number is created from its three components (H, T and U), ask the class to see if the place value significance is understood (for example ask what the value of the middle digit is before sliding this card away from the cluster.
● Try with other numbers if time allows.

Group work
● Explain that the group will be playing a game to try to make the largest total of two numbers, using 'special' number dice to help. Show the two dice to be used and the cards from an enlarged version of photocopiable page 41.
● Select a volunteer to roll the dice, say the number they have created and then represent that number using the appropriate place value cards.
● Ask: *Would someone like to roll the dice to try and beat this total?* Overlap and then partition the place value cards after each turn to reinforce the value of the digits within any given two-digit arrangement.

Paired work
● Provide each pair of children with the prepared dice, and give each child a set of cards (from photocopiable page 41). Explain how to play the game:
  - Each player rolls the dice and creates a two-digit number with the appropriate cards.
  - They throw again, recording the outcomes in the form of an addition sum. Place value cards may only be used once (so the children may need to throw again). This is an important feature as it limits the maximum total to 99.
● Deconstruct the addition problem by grouping the two tens cards together first and calculating the total. Add the units together and consequently find and record the overall total.
● Promote the idea that most people find it easier to deal with the tens digits first when adding two-digit numbers, as these are the most significant.

Plenary
● After several turns ask the children to identify the highest number they have recorded. Compare all the children's results to see who achieved the highest number overall. A good visual way to do this is to ask all the children to write their names on sticky notes and then fix them over the appropriate cells on a hundred-square.

Potential difficulties	Further support
Some children may experience difficulties in re-grouping the sub-totals into tens and ones.	Be clear to use language which is familiar to the children and consistent with school policy (especially the choice between the words 'units' and 'ones').

Top totals

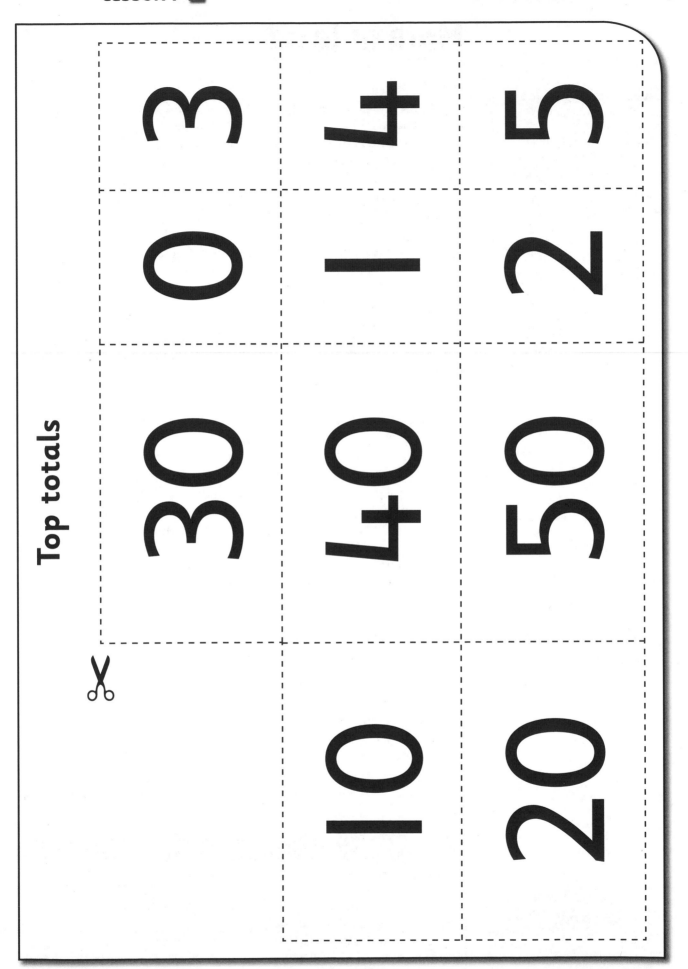

3	0	30	10
4	1	40	
5	2	50	20

More or less?

Learning Objectives
(Y2) Use and begin to read the vocabulary of comparing and ordering numbers, including ordinal numbers to 100. Use the = sign to represent equality. **(Y3)** Read and begin to write the vocabulary of comparing and ordering numbers, including ordinal numbers to at least 100. **(Y4)** Read and write the vocabulary of comparing and ordering numbers. **Use symbols correctly, including less than (<), greater than (>), equals (=).**

Mental Starter
See the starter activity, 'Lots of numbers' on page 12.

You will need
Photocopiable page 43 (enlarged and backed if preferred); a pointer (plastic disposable stirrer or similar); counters; a demonstration 100 square; two sticky notes; large standard dice (Whole class section only).

Moving on
● Modify the centre of the resource sheet, replacing *is more than* with *is less than*. Play as before.
● Work with larger numbers, possibly written on the faces of two blank dice.
● Ask the children to record each winning sequence, and consider introducing the symbols < and >.

Whole class work
● Arrange five cards, depicting a range of two-digit numbers. Include a pairing such as 34 and 43, where the digits are the same.
● Invite the class to identify the smallest and then the largest number in the collection. Follow this by asking which number should go in the central position. At this stage of the discussion, you might discuss the significance of the two numbers containing identical digits. Throughout the task, use the language of comparison (for example, more/less). Finish the activity by allocating the second and fourth placed numbers.
● If time allows, repeat with another set of five two-digit numbers.

Group work
● Revisit the terms *more than* and *less than*. If necessary, make a comparison between two numbers along a number line.
● Encourage each child to verbalise two statements (each time using the same two random numbers) with one statement incorporating *more than*; the other *less than*.

Paired work
● Review the numbers on the photocopiable game board. Read the words in the centre, *is more than* together.
● Use a disposable coffee stirrer (or similar item, with a hole) to act as a pointer. Locate the hole over the centre of the target and hold it in place with a pencil point. Flick the stirrer to simulate a random number generator!
● The children should use the pointer to generate a number on each target board and then make a statement, such as: *76 is more than 72*. For each statement that is actually correct, they receive a counter.
● Players take turns to play, and the game is over when one player wins the agreed number of counters. Ensure winning statements are read out fully (using the correct terminology) before awarding counters.
● The boards have been designed with a 50 per cent success rate.

Plenary
● Provide a demonstration 100 square. Be ready with two sticky notes labelled *more than* and *less than*. With a secret number in mind, ask: *What is my number?* As you get responses, place the *more than* and *less than* labels over the selected numbers. This sets the boundaries of the range and serves to keep track of subsequent guesses. As the group refine their guesses, the two sticky notes should shuffle towards each other until a correct guess is achieved. Encourage the children to sample the vocabulary of comparison, rather than simply calling out numbers.

Potential difficulties	Further support
The children have trouble visualising the numbers.	Refer back to a number line to visually reference the numbers for counting.
The pointer may prove impractical for children with poor motor skills.	Suitably labelled blank dice could be substituted, perhaps with a narrower range of numbers as appropriate.

Name _____

More or less?

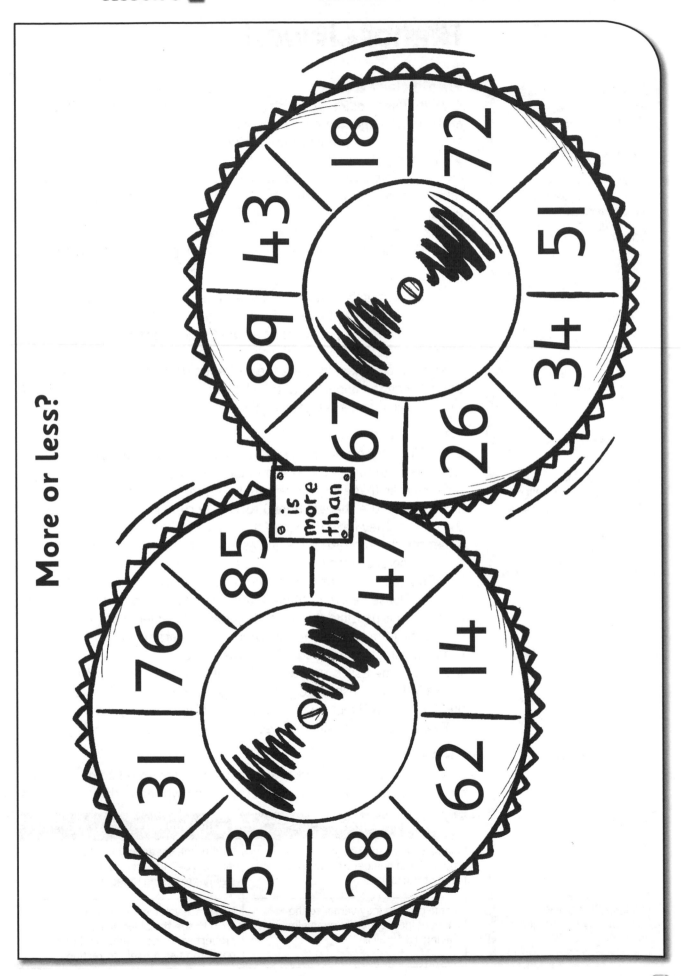

is more than

Higher...lower!

Learning Objectives
(Y2) Compare two given two-digit numbers, say which is more or less, and give a number which lies between them.
(Y3) Compare two given three-digit numbers, say which is more or less, and give a number which lies between them.
(Y4) Give one or more numbers lying between two given numbers and order a set of whole numbers less than 10,000.

Mental Starter
See the starter activity, 'Guess my word' on page 12.

You will need
Two numeral dice labelled 1, 2, 4, 6, 8, 9 and 1, 2, 3, 5, 7, 8; photocopiable page 45 (one per child); individual whiteboards.

Whole class work
● Invite three volunteers to play a game involving making and then ordering two-digit numbers. Each person takes a turn to roll a large standard dice. They must record their outcome as either a ten or a unit.
● Given that the aim is to make a large two-digit number, a low outcome is typically best allocated as a units digit. Each player then takes a second turn, inserting that outcome in the remaining (tens or units) space.
● The whole class can review the 'scores' and arrange in ascending order. Use the vocabulary of comparison throughout, such as *more/less*.

Group work
● Let group members take turns to generate a two-digit number by throwing the dice and sliding the two together in the order of their choosing. Write the outcomes as a two-digit number on individual whiteboards, together with the child's name.
● As turns are taken, arrange the whiteboards in ascending numerical order, taking the opportunity to talk about numbers being *more* and *less* than certain numbers created earlier.

Paired work
● In pairs, let the children take turns to roll both dice and align them side by side to form a two-digit number. Provide a photocopiable sheet for each child (page 45). Explain that the range of each string of beads illustrated on the sheet is from 0 to 100. Encourage each child to record the number they have thrown in the most appropriate space.
● Let the children take turns and ask them to continue to fill empty spaces wherever possible. If a number cannot be placed, that turn is lost. Play continues until one player is able to fill every bead with a number. Please be aware that although there are many combinations of numbers, it is possible that a poorly-judged placement can prevent the child completing the chain. If this becomes apparent, an earlier decision can be modified at the discretion of the adult.
● As play progresses, encourage the children to verbalise their moves, particularly with respect to the language of comparison. Encourage prediction – ask: *What number would you like to get to fill that bead?*
● Play a new game using the second string of beads.

Plenary
● Return to the group work, this time using three standard dice to create and order three-digit numbers on their whiteboards.

Moving on
● Modify the sheet by changing the two beads labelled as '100' to '1000'.
● Provide a third dice with a selection of single digit numbers. Play as earlier, this time ordering three-digit numbers.

Potential difficulties	Further support
Some children may be insecure with the order of numbers in the upper end of the range.	Modify the sheet and use dice labelled 0–5 to order numbers in the newly-prescribed range of 0 to 55.
Some children may verbalise the number incorrectly (for example, saying 18 for 81).	Use place value cards to allow the child to see the place value properties of the number and to give opportunities for self-correction.

Higher...lower!

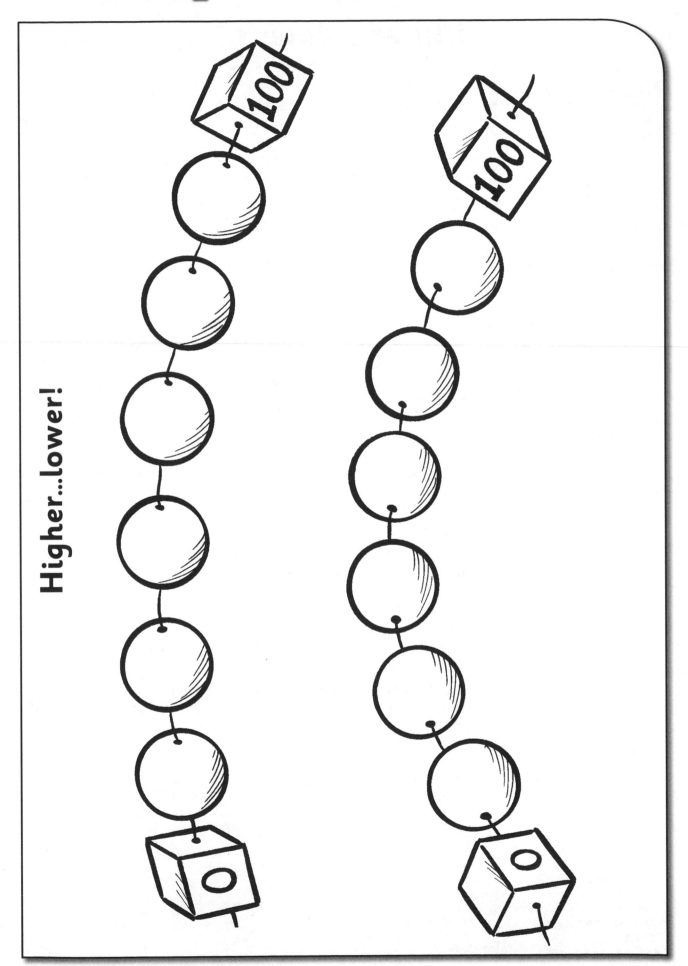

Ups and downs

Learning Objectives
(Y2) Say the number that is 1 or 10 more or less than any given two-digit number.
(Y3) Say the number that is 1, 10 or 100 more or less than any given two- or three-digit number.
(Y4) Count on or back in repeated steps of 1, 10 or 100.

Mental Starter
See the starter activity, 'Guess my sum' on page 13.

You will need
Card copies of photocopiable page 47 (one per pair), cut out to create 20 individual cards; 100 square.

Whole class work
● Starting at zero, chant the sequence of numbers generated by counting in steps of 100. Explore what happens after 900, crossing the thousand boundary.
● Repeat the above, starting from any two-digit number.
● Beginning with a number close to 1000, count back in steps of 100.

Group work
● Provide a demonstration 100 square. Identify a number then find a number which is 10 more. On a standard grid, the children can be shown that this is the number below (in the same column). Similarly, reference to the number above will show the idea of 10 less.

Paired work
● Shuffle, then arrange the 20 cards face down in a 'five by four' array. Explain that the task is to find 10 pairs of cards where one card is 10 more/less than the other.
● Revise the concept of 10 more/less with reference back to a 100 square, moving down/up a column to identify comparative numbers.
● Now ask the first child to randomly turn two of the cards over to identify if they have a difference of 10. If so, the child must say: 'x is ten more than y', or 'y is ten less than x'. If the chosen pair is not complementary in this respect, the cards are turned over. Play continues until all 10 pairs have been established. The winner is the child with the most cards.

Plenary
● To conclude the task, group the children together again. Engage them in arranging the cards in ascending numerical order and review again those cards with a difference of 10.
● If time/ability allows, provide some extra blank cards and invite individuals to first think of a number which is 10 more/fewer than one of those already represented, then place that number in the appropriate position of the developing number line.

Moving on
● Let the children develop their own set of cards using the same structure as the original photocopiable sheet.
● Modify the resource to include numbers which extend beyond 100.
● Modify the resource to sample the higher order objective of saying a number which is 100 more/less than another given number.

Potential difficulties	Further support
Inability to cope with 10 more/less without significant support.	Consider modifying the resource to find pairs with a difference of just one (one more/less).
Some children will be confident in talking about a given number being ten more than another, but will find it hard to switch the numbers around when using the term 'is 10 less than'.	Reference to the 100 square will help the children to understand the concept as it provides a useful visual model.

Ups and downs

56	62	4	19	41
29	75	90	57	33
67	51	88	72	78
23	46	14	80	65

Take three

Learning Objectives
(Y2) Order whole numbers to at least 100, and position them on a number line and 100-square.
(Y3) Order whole numbers to at least 1000, and position them on a number line.

Mental Starter
See the starter activity, 'Make it up' on page 13.

You will need
Photocopiable page 49 copied onto card (to create at least one set of cards per pair); prepare a 0-500 number line (with hundreds marked) and copy for each pair; individual whiteboards.

Whole class work
● Arrange five cards, depicting a range of three-digit numbers. Include a pairing such as 562 and 526, where the digits are the same.
● Invite the class to identify the smallest and then the largest number in the collection. Then ask which number should go in the central position. At this stage, you might discuss the significance of the two numbers containing common digits; throughout, use the language of comparison. Finish by allocating the second and fourth placed numbers.

Group work
● Ask the children to create a three-digit number using the numerals 1, 2 and 3 in any order. Let them record it on their whiteboards. Compare all the suggestions in terms of greater/less than and arrange the outcomes in ascending order.
● Finally, ask: *Are there any combinations missing?* (There should be six unique combinations.)

Paired work
● Cut out the cards from page 49 and shuffle them. Ask a child to take three cards and form a three-digit number. Point out that the inclusion of the digit '4' enables a wider range of numbers to be sampled. This task can also involve two or more of the same digit (such as 244).
● After saying the number formed, let the child write it in the appropriate place on a 0-500 number line. Play proceeds with each child taking it in turns to take three cards from the pack, form their numbers, then write them on the number line (each child should write in a different colour so as to identify their own numbers). When the pack is exhausted, reshuffle the cards and continue.
● The objective of the game can be based on securing the highest number by the end of the activity, or having the largest range from smallest to largest number.
● Throughout the activity, help the children to use the language of ordering and comparison. Ask questions such as: *What is the largest number you could make?*; *Is that number more than that one?*

Plenary
● Review the outcomes recorded on the number line. Discuss the value of specific digits, to ensure that the children are thinking in terms of place value.

Moving on
● Extend the range of numbers by adding or replacing digits greater than four, modifying the photocopiable pages accordingly.

Potential difficulties	Further support
Numbers such as 421 and 412 may be confused both in relation to how they are spoken and where they are mutually located.	Encourage precision of speech, with attention to how the words are distinctly different in sound.
A number which includes the digit 4 might initially be seen as being greater than a number without (such as 244 over 311).	Draw attention to the place value of each digit.

Take three

2	1	4	3	2	1
4	3	2	1	4	3
2	1	4	3	2	1
4	3	2	1	4	3

In its place

Learning Objectives
(Y2) Order whole numbers to at least 100, and position them on a number line and 100 square.
(Y3) Order whole numbers to at least 1000, and position them on a number line.

Mental Starter
See the starter activity, 'Combinations' on page 13.

You will need:
Photocopiable page 51 (one per child); 10 counters per pair; whiteboard.

Whole class work
- Provide three digits and invite the class to make the largest possible number. Explore the value of each digit within that number. Next, establish the smallest possible number the class can make and, as before, explore place value.
- Extend this activity by exploring what numbers can be generated within the range that has been established. If all three digits are different, there will be a further four numbers to be generated. Then ask the class to arrange these in ascending order.

Group work
- Present several random numbers (0–500) on a whiteboard. Ask the children to identify the smallest in the range.
- Next, ask questions such as: *Which number is the closest to this one?; How do you know?* Continue with similar questions until all the numbers are in ascending order.
- Only move on if the children are able to order numbers in this range, and have a clear understanding of the significance of place value.

Paired work
- Prepare a set of 20 cards using photocopiable page 51. Explain to the children that they're going to try to put the numbers they choose in order.
- Invite each child to make a line of 10 counters, regularly spaced, to simulate a number line. Explain that they will make a number sequence in ascending order from left to right, with numbers within the range 0 to 500 (actually 22 to 472).
- The children take it in turns to choose a card from the top of the shuffled pile. They must decide where that number will be best placed over a counter. The children continue to take turns, trying to add cards in numerical order – where a number cannot be placed, because there is no counter to locate it appropriately, it must be kept to one side as a 'discard'. Once a card has been committed to a counter, its position cannot be shifted.
- Talk to the children at suitable points in order to ascertain their understanding and capability. Ask, for example: *What number could go in-between these two numbers?; Is your number more than that one?*
- Play continues until all the cards have been taken (10 per child). The winner is the player with fewest cards discarded.

Plenary
- Talk about strategies for deciding where to place cards. In addition, talk about how a growing knowledge of the cards in the pack, and an awareness of what cards have been selected by both players, can influence where particular cards should be placed.

Moving On
- Extend the range of numbers up to 1000. For a regular set in the range 50–1000 inclusive, feature every multiple of 50 therein; for a random set modify each card to a 'near multiple of 50'.

Potential difficulties	Further support
The random nature of the cards and the range of numbers sampled may be too difficult to enable attempts at ordering.	Replace the cards with a set of twenty in the range 5–100 inclusive, featuring every multiple of 5 therein.

In its place

108	97	71	54	22
212	201	173	137	128
366	342	307	281	262
472	446	437	417	383

Round up?

Learning Objectives
(Y2) Round numbers less than 100 to the nearest 10. **(Y3)** Round any two-digit number to the nearest 10 and any three-digit number to the nearest 100.

Mental Starter
See the starter activity, 'More combinations' on page 14.

You will need
Photocopiable page 53 (one per three children); two numeral dice labelled 1, 3, 5, 5, 7, 9 and 2, 4, 5, 5, 6, 8; coins (in denominations of 10 and 1); coloured counters (in three different colours); 100 grid (Whole class section only).

Whole class work

● Identify any number on the 100 square and ask the class which multiple of 10 it is nearest to. You might, at this stage, want to clarify where on the grid the multiples of 10 lie.

● Confirm the nearest 10 by counting on and back to the multiple of 10 both after and before. With the exception of multiples of 5, it will become apparent when it is best to round up from a number, and when to round down.

● Teach the convention for multiples of 5 where, unless otherwise stated, the rounded multiple of 10 is found by *counting on*.

Group work

● Present an amount of money or any number less than 100, where the number of units is less than five (presented in tens and ones if money).

● Ask the children which is the nearest multiple of 10.

● Repeat with another amount, this time with the units greater than five. Explore the distinction between rounding up or down. Finally select a number with a unit value of 5 and ask which multiple of 10 is the nearest. As there is no difference up or down, it is necessary to teach the children that the convention is to round up (but there are occasions in real life where we might do either).

Individual/paired work

● Provide a copy of photocopiable page 53 for each child, pair or group of three. The children take turns to roll both dice and then push the dice together to form a two-digit number. Ask the child to decide which multiple of ten their two-digit number is closest to. If such a multiple of ten has not been previously occupied on the photocopiable sheet, that child can claim it by placing a coloured counter of their choice onto it. Play continues until all the spaces are occupied – the winner being the player having used the most counters.

● Note that the dice have both been 'loaded' to encourage the use of two-digit numbers ending in 5, in order to reinforce the convention for rounding such outcomes up to the next multiple of 10.

Plenary

● Talk through any strategies that have been identified. For example, the chance of occupying the 100 space is significantly less than, say, securing the 60 location. Therefore if a 9 and a 5 is achieved as a dice outcome, it should not be 'wasted' on 59 in preference to 95.

Potential difficulties	Further support
The dice do not afford a visual image of the number's positional significance.	Use a number line or number square if necessary, to give a visual model of rounding to the nearest multiple of 10.

Moving On
● Use three standard dice and work on rounding up/down to the nearest 100 in the range 100–700.

Round up?

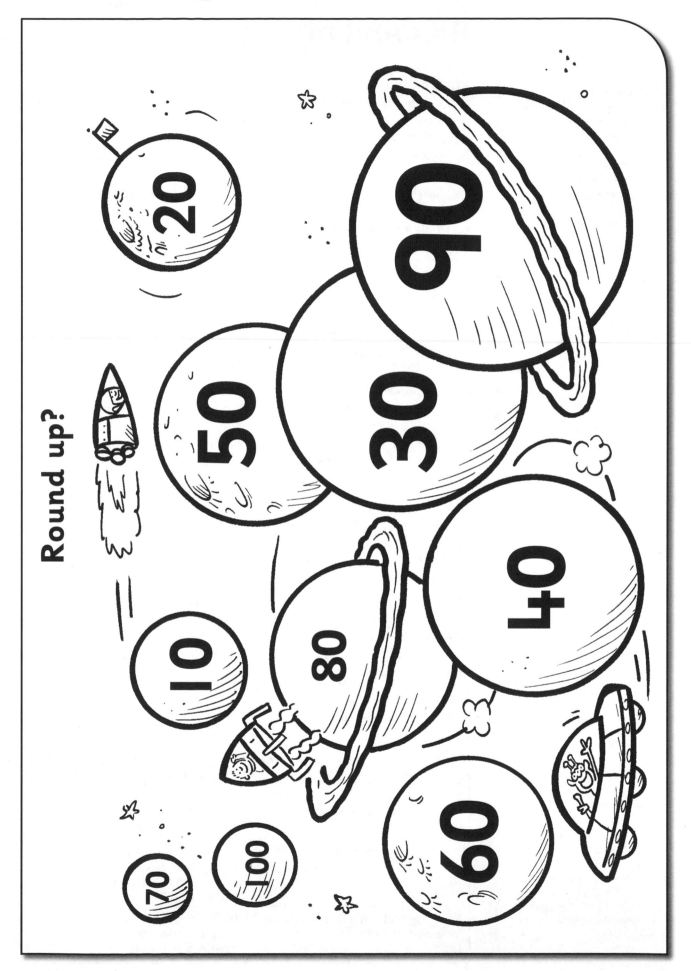

Bits and pieces

Learning Objectives
(Y2) Begin to recognise and find one half and one quarter of shapes and small numbers of objects.
(Y3) Recognise unit fractions such as 1/2, 1/3, 1/4, 1/5, 1/10 and use them to find fractions of shapes and numbers.

Mental Starter
See the starter activity, 'Bugs' on page 14.

You will need
Card copies of photocopiable page 55; cubes/counters (for calculation); a tall pot; 24 sorting objects.

Whole class work
● Present a range of numbers (multiples of 4) and ask the children to halve them. Explore the way that halving again gives a number representing a quarter the value of the original number.
● Show this diagrammatically with a circle containing the original number. Draw a semi-circle and enter a number which is half that amount. Finally record the appropriate number in a sketch of a quarter of a circle.
● If time and capability allows, the exercise could be extended with diagrammatic versions of multiples of 8, with whole circles diminishing to a section representing one-eighth.

Group work
● Provide a set of 24 objects for sorting. Use these to find unit fractions of that amount (such as 1/2 , 1/3, 1/4, 1/8).
● Demonstrate two distinct strategies for arriving at answers:
  - Share the objects into equal subsets as one might deal a pack of cards;
  - Take every second/third/fourth/eighth object in the count of all the objects, in accordance with the fraction sought.
● In the activity that follows, the quantities of numbers, and their fractions have been pre-determined to give only whole number answers.

Individual work
● Place a prepared set of fraction strips, cut from photocopiable page 55, in a tall pot to allow for random selection.
● Ask the child to select a strip and read the information (such as a quarter of 12). Invite him or her to use cubes or counters as necessary to solve the problem by counting out the objects and then, when looking at quarters of quantities for example, partitioning into four equal subsets.
● After each calculation, the links between multiplication, division and repeated addition can be made.

Plenary
● Review the answers to each of the fraction strips. Ask questions such as: *Which strip gives the highest/lowest number of objects?*

Potential difficulties	Further support
Some children will be unfamiliar with fractions other than one half and one quarter.	Demonstrate each unit fraction using a fraction wall where the lengths are common.
The uniform length of the strips might cause confusion for some children.	Create pieces which are proportional in length (for example, the number depicted on the strip can be used to form its length).
Some may feel that unit fractions increase as the denominator gets larger.	Demonstrate each unit fraction using a fraction wall where the lengths are common.

Moving On
● Extend the range of unit fractions by creating additional challenges.
● Begin to explore beyond unit fractions (for example, three-quarters).

Bits and pieces

$\frac{1}{2}$		⑫

$\frac{1}{4}$				⑫

$\frac{1}{3}$			⑫

$\frac{1}{6}$						⑫

$\frac{1}{2}$		⑳

$\frac{1}{4}$				⑫

$\frac{1}{5}$					⑳

$\frac{1}{10}$										⑳

$\frac{1}{2}$		⑳

$\frac{1}{4}$				⑫

$\frac{1}{8}$								⑫

Words worth

Learning Objectives
(Y2) Extend understanding of the operations of addition and subtraction. Use and begin to read the related vocabulary.
(Y3) Extend understanding of the operations of addition and subtraction, read and begin to write the related vocabulary.

Mental Starter
See the starter activity, 'Partners' on page 14.

You will need
Photocopiable page 57; a home-made, long-numbered track up to 50 spaces from start to finish with a star sticker every third space; a playing piece for each child; a standard dice; a whiteboard.

Whole class work

● Present a selection of mathematical questions using the following words and phrases; *sum, total, difference, how many altogether, how many more, subtract less*.
● Ask the class which words gave clues about the mathematical operation required and how the answer was calculated mentally.
● Invite the children to create a class number story using mathematical vocabulary; the story might connect to a theme, which is being developed in another subject area.
● Pay particular attention to the key words and phrases used.

Group work

● Write a selection of words and phrases associated with the operations of addition (such as: *total*) and subtraction (such as: *how many more?*) onto a whiteboard.
● Together, sort the words and phrases into those for addition and those for subtraction.
● Select one phrase or word at a time and engage the group in using the words in a number problem of their own creation.

Paired work (can also be played with up to 4 players)

● Cut out all 12 cards from photocopiable page 57, shuffle and place them face down in a pack. Give each child a playing piece and show them the prepared game track.
● Let the children take turns to roll a single (standard) dice. Ask each child to predict where they will stop before they count on the required amount. If the child 'lands' on a star, the player will only be able to move on their next turn if they answer the card taken from the top of the stack of cards. A failed attempt means waiting a turn and answering a fresh question. When the stack is exhausted, the cards are reshuffled and used again.

Plenary

● Review each one of the cards used for the task. Sort the cards into those for addition and those for subtraction, or put the cards in ascending order based on their numerical outcomes.

Potential difficulties	Further support
Some children may be unfamiliar with some of the language which is sampled.	Develop word banks progressively as they arise, to support the identification of prompts for addition or subtraction.
Some may read *How many more?* as a cue for addition (owing to the first two words suggesting addition).	(As above)
The child's use of the word 'difference' may relate only to everyday experience (such as comparing two objects).	(As above) Provide real objects for calculation.

Moving On
● Extend the range of vocabulary sampled on the cards and/or increase the range of numbers.

Words worth

What is the total of six and seven?	**How many more is 11 than 7?**	**Take 6 from 11.**
What is 4 more than 12?	**16 less 7.**	**What is eight plus five?**
		15 subtract 6.
The sum of 9 and 5.	**What is the difference between 16 and 8?**	**What must you add to 7 to make 12?**
		Add 12 to 5.
		How much more is 18 than 9?

Which way now?

Learning Objectives
(Y2) Understand that more than two numbers can be added.
(Y3) Extend understanding that more than two numbers can be added.

Mental Starter
See the starter activity, 'Calculator patterns' on page 15.

You will need
Copies of photocopiable page 59; counters.

Whole class work
● Present the numbers 12, 16 and 18 and explain that there are many ways of finding their total. Ask the class if they think different methods of calculation might give a different answer (which clearly it shouldn't!).
● Tell the class that you would like to try this out. Invite individual children to suggest methods and follow these through with calculation.
● If this method has not already been covered, explore the 'convenient' pairing of 12 and 18, leading to a multiple of 10. Such a total then makes it relatively easy to add on 16, to give a total of 46.

Group work
● Present three number cards from page 59, the 3, 5 and 7. Tell the group that you are going to add these numbers in as many different ways as possible. Engage them in finding and recording all six possible number sentences (for example, 3 + 7 + 5) without, at this stage, calculating the (common) total.
● Ask: *Which sentence will give the greatest total?* This will confirm whether or not an appreciation of conservation is emerging. Work through each number sentence (from left to right in each case) and ask: *Which number sentence is the easiest to calculate?* You may choose to explore some of the strategies suggested in the next section.

Paired work
● Let the children take turns to select three numeral cards at random (pre-cut from photocopiable page 59). Ask the children to arrange their cards on the table and consider how to add the three numbers together in a way which seems 'efficient'. Possible strategies include:
- adding on a small number to a large number;
- selecting two identical numbers first in order to apply knowledge of doubles;
- establishing two numbers with a total of 10;
- adding two numbers which are both '5 and a bit'.
● To make the task more competitive, a child may collect a counter if they secure the higher total on that turn. Play continues until one player has collected a pre-determined number of counters. As the stack is exhausted, the cards are re-shuffled.

Plenary
● Review some of the 'convenient' pairings available from the pack of cards. Consider which strategies proved to be most helpful to each individual.

Moving On
● If the activity is to be made competitive, a tally of points 'earned' can be made with the use of counting apparatus (such as base 10) up to a predetermined target total.
● Modify the photocopiable sheet to include larger numbers with scope for pairings totalling 20 and/or larger doubles.

Potential difficulties	Further support
Mental facility alone may not offer enough support.	Provide real objects or number lines for calculation.
Counting on may erroneously include the number being added to, thus giving an incorrect answer.	Putting the first number 'in the head' (touch head with one hand) and counting out the number to be added (other hand).

Which way now?

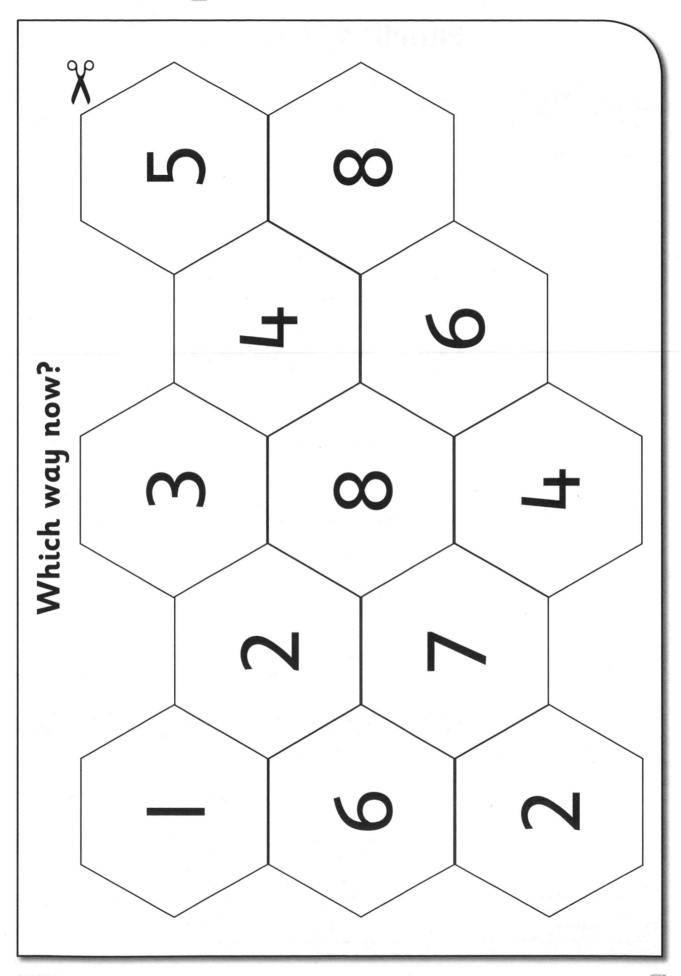

Families

Learning Objectives
(Y2) Understand that subtraction is the inverse of addition (subtraction reverses addition).
(Y3) Extend understanding that subtraction is the inverse of addition.

Mental Starter
See the starter activity, 'Calculator patterns (2)' on page 15.

You will need
Photocopiable page 61; a demonstration number line; individual number lines; counters.

Whole class work
- Present the class with the number sentence 34 + 17 = 51.
- Invite the class to give related verbal statements relating to this (for example 51 is 17 more than 34).
- Establish the fact that related sentences sometimes sample the language of subtraction. Make a collection of mathematical words and phrases sampled through such discussion.

Group work
- Show adding one number to another as a physical action by counting on along a demonstration number line. Ask: *Where did we start?* and *How many did we add on?* Repeat the activity several times.
- When the children are confident with this process, ask them how they might 'undo' the addition of a number. Record the number sentences for the example you are working on: 6 + 4 = 10 and 10 – 4 = 6.
- Next, consider the other number sentences in the 'family'. For example, ask: *How could we get an answer of 10 if we started at 4?*

Individual work
- Prepare a copy of photocopiable page 61 for each child by cutting up the three sections and creating the number cards. Give each child the set of number cards and the number sentence template section.
- Sort the numeral cards into three sets and ask: *Can you use one number from each pile to fill the first empty number sentence?* Support as necessary and compare (potentially different) answers (for example: 5 + 6 = 11 and 6 + 5 = 11). Continue in a similar way, using number lines or counters as required, to detail the two subtraction statements.
- Now challenge the children to select three different numbers, filling out the empty grid section. Repeat the activity above, reinforcing the idea of number families.

Plenary
- Look at the different number facts sampled by individuals and reinforce the *commutative* aspect of addition (this term does not need to be known by children at this stage).

Potential difficulties	Further support
Counting on/back strategies may still include the first number as part of that count.	Locate the first number 'in the head' (some children find it helpful to link this to the physical action of touching the head with one hand and then counting on/back with the other).
Some children may think reversals are acceptable in subtraction (such as: 6 – 11 = 5 when the required sentence is 11 – 6 = 5).	Stress the importance of conventions for subtraction (when a positive answer is the required outcome). Where order is not specifically required the concept is that of *difference*.

Moving On
- Provide a further blank grid to allow free choice in creating a number family.
- Extend the notion of inverse operations to link multiplication and division.

Families

6	5	11
6	5	11
6	5	11
6	5	11

Full score

Learning Objectives
(Y2) Know by heart all pairs of numbers with a total of 20 (such as, 13 + 7, 6 + 14). **(Y3) Know by heart all addition and subtraction facts for each number to 20.**

Mental Starter
See the starter activity, 'Even sort' on page 15.

You will need
Photocopiable page 63 (one copy per pair); counting objects or number lines.

Whole class work
● Tell the class that you have added two numbers and have made a total of 20. Invite them to guess what the two numbers might have been and record their suggestions.
● As the opportunity arises, focus on how the modification of one sentence can generate another (for example 14 + 6 can be modified to 13 add 7 by 'shifting' one unit from the 14 to the 6.)

Group work
● Revise knowledge of number bonds of 10, initially using 'quick-fire' questions.
● If the children are clearly struggling with this work then consider reducing the range of numbers tackled in the next section (from 1 to 19, down to 1 to 9, with an additional card depicting 5).
● Talk about suitable strategies such as starting with the larger number and counting on. Encourage the children to relate one number fact to another (for example, 6 + 4 gives the same total as 5 + 5 because the 6 compensates for the fact that 4 is one less than 5).
● Move on to revise knowledge of bonds for 20, using known facts to find solutions not immediately known (for example, 7 + 3 = 10 may support the fact that 17 + 3 = 20).

Paired work
● Prepare and shuffle the set of 20 cards and arrange them face down on the table in an array of 4 rows of 5. Invite the children, in pairs, to take it in turns to select any two cards in an attempt to make a total of 20. If the cards give any total other than 20, they should be returned to their original positions.
● Note that the cards include visual images which offer some support for calculation. The shaded arrangement of dots means that a successful pairing would result in all 20 dots being 'filled up'. If required, offer further physical aids such as a bead string or 0–20 number line.
● Play continues with players collecting successful pairings. The winner is the player with the most cards when all 10 pairs have been taken.

Plenary
● Work with the whole group and pair the cards again. Arrange them as a sequence (1 and 19; 2 and 18; 3 and 17 and so on).
● Demonstrate the links with bonds of 10 (1 and 9; 2 and 8; 3 and 7 and so on).

Moving On
● Provide a selection of cards giving pairs of numbers for a different given total (such as bonds of 50).

Potential difficulties	Further support
Some children may find the activity too hard as it calls on visual memory as well as skills of calculation.	The cards can be arranged face-up for selection.
There may be insufficient confidence to manage bonds of 20.	Reduce the number of cards to include only those giving totals of 10.

Full score

Round we go

Whole class work
- Provide a range of 'quick fire' questions featuring addition (maximum total 20).
- Repeat for subtraction.
- Discuss how knowledge of an addition fact (such as 9 + 8 = 17) can help with related subtraction problems (in this case a question such as 17 – 8 = ?).
- Discuss strategies for quick calculation such as bridging through 10 and recognising near doubles.

Group work
- Work with groups of up to five children. Take just a few of the cards (pre-cut from activity sheet 65) to sample both addition and subtraction.
- Explain that you would like the children to explain their strategies and give solutions as they work. Use individual whiteboards if you wish to assess individuals' readiness to work without support.
- Shuffle the cards and share them out amongst the group. Ask each child to place their cards face up for all to see. Select any child to start, by asking what the answer is to one of their cards. When a correct solution is given, say 16, ask the whole group to check to see if the number 16 is on any of their cards. Whoever has the number is the next person to have a turn, using the identified card.
- Take time to share the calculations with the group and encourage them to share suitable strategies. Play continues until all the problems have been sampled – this will also take the group back to the beginning of the loop.
- If time allows, collect and redistribute the cards and play again.

Plenary
- Review some of the cards again, this time looking at how some subtraction problems can be 'undone' by reference to the associated addition problem. For example – 'I know that 19 subtract 8 is 11 because 11 add 8 equals 19.'

Potential difficulties	Further support
Counting on/back strategies may still include the first number as part of that count.	Locate the first number 'in the head' (some children find it helpful to link this to the physical action of touching the head with one hand and then counting on/back with the other).
The range of numbers may be too high.	Create a reduced set of cards where each answer from 1 to 10 is sampled. Also ensure that the operation on the final card results in an answer which 'loops back' to the number presented on the first card.

Round we go

3 add 14	**10** subtract 7	**6** add 4
8 add 4	**4** add 4	**9** subtract 5
19 subtract 8	**16** add 3	**7** add 9
15 add 5	**1** add 14	**5** subtract 4
18 subtract 4	**2** add 16	**13** subtract 11

14 subtract 8		
17 subtract 8		
12 subtract 5		
11 subtract 6		
20 subtract 7		

Top up

Learning Objectives
(Y2) Know by heart all pairs of multiples of 10 with a total of 100 (such as 30 + 70).
(Y3) Derive quickly all pairs of multiples of 5 with a total of 100 (such as 35 + 65).

Mental Starter
See the starter activity, 'Two-times table' on page 16.

You will need
Photocopiable page 67 (paper or card copy for each small group); 100-square (for demonstration).

Whole class work
● Revise counting in tens to 100. Ask the children to use fingers to show 3 tens and ask for the value (30). In this example, ask how many more tens are needed to make 100. The use of fingers to represent tens enables the children to use complements to 10 in solving such problems.
● Go around the class counting in fives from 0, extending a little way beyond 100.
● Provide a multiple of 5 ending in 5 (for example 35) and ask how many to the next multiple of 10 (5). Follow this by asking how many more tens are needed to make 100. Again, the use of fingers enables counting on in tens to that figure.

Group work
● Count in tens using a 100-square as a visual prompt. Repeat for the multiples of 5, paying particular attention to the spatial nature of the 'stations' on the 100-square.
● Use the 100-square to assist with counting on from multiples of 10 and then multiples of 5. If children find it too difficult to find complementary pairs of multiples of 5 (with a total of 100), consider reducing the number of cards in the activity to follow (see Potential difficulties, below).

Paired work
● Prepare and shuffle the set of 20 cards from photocopiable page 67 and arrange them face down on the table in an array of 4 rows of 5. The two players must take turns to select any two cards in an attempt to make a total of 100. If the cards give any total other than 100 they should be returned to their original position.
● Point out the way that the grids are shaded on the cards. Demonstrate how this helps with the calculations. If required, use further aids such as a 100-square.
● Play continues with players collecting successful pairings. The winner is the player with the most cards when all 10 pairs have been taken.

Plenary
● Write down some successful pairings of numbers with a total of 100.
● With multiples of 10, reinforce the idea that the number of tens (the tens digits) always total 10 (such as **7**0 + **3**0 = 100).
● With multiples of 5 ending in 5, exemplify how the tens digits total 9 (which is then 'topped up' to 10 with two further 5s). For example: **6**5 + **3**5 = 100.

Moving On
● Try creating a complementary set (for totals of 100) using pairings sampling all unit digits (such as 74 and 26).

Potential difficulties	Further support
Some children may find the activity too hard as it calls on visual memory, as well as skills of calculation.	The cards can be arranged face-up for selection.
Complementary multiples of 5 ending in 5 may prove too difficult.	Reduce the number of cards to those depicting multiples of 10 only.

Top up

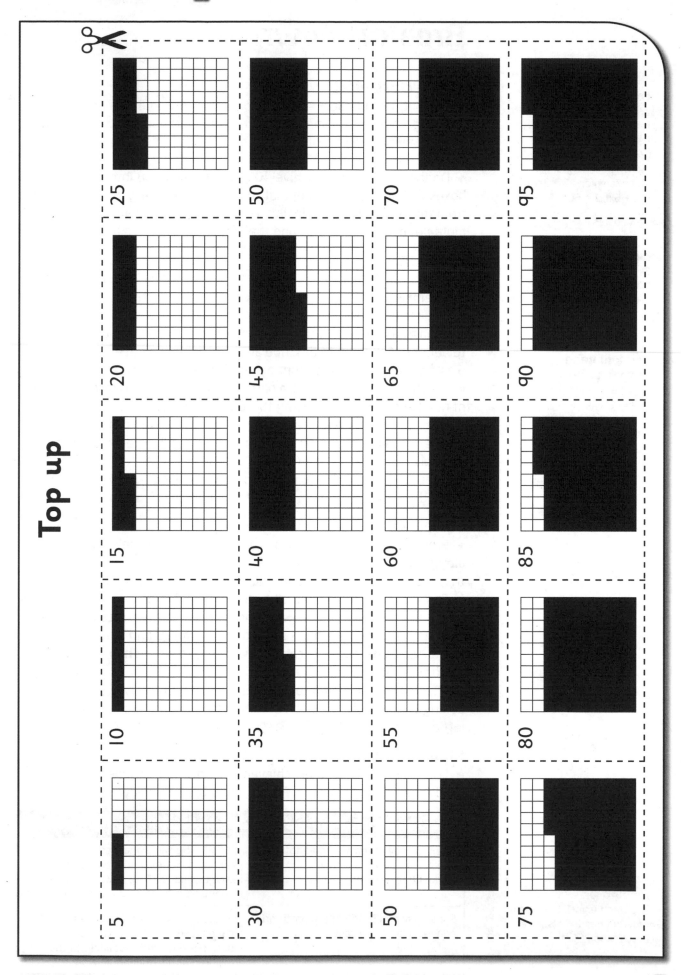

Break it down

Learning Objectives
(Y2) Partition additions into tens and units, then recombine.
(Y3) Partition into '5 and a bit' when adding 6, 7, 8 or 9 (For example, 47 + 8 = 45 + 2 + 5 + 3 = 50 + 5 = 55).

Mental Starter
See the starter activity, 'Five-times table' on page 16.

You will need
Photocopiable page 69 (one copy per group); two dice labelled 5, 8, 10, 13, 15, 18 and 6, 7, 11, 12, 16, 17; interlocking cubes in two colours.

Whole class work
- Present the sum 38 + 45 and explain that the total will be found by breaking down both numbers. Begin by drawing two boxes underneath the first number. Ask for that number to be split into tens and units to give 30 and 8.
- Do the same with 45 to give 40 and 5. Break the 8 into two further boxes of 5 and 3, explaining that this will make it 'easy' to add to the 5 from the other numbers. Finally, solve the problem by adding the multiples of 10, the two 5s and the remaining 3 to give a total of 83.

Group work
- Provide each child with a tower of 10 interlocking cubes, using two differently-coloured towers of 5 to emphasise the idea of this as a useful 'staging post'.
- In pairs, ask one child to create a tower of 7 cubes and the other a tower of 8. Ask them to describe any strategies they used. Did they use 5 as a starting point and count on, or did they count out all the cubes?
- Explain the value of using a partitioning strategy and record a series of number sentences involving this partitioning. For example, 7 = 5 + 2.
- Next, demonstrate (practically, using cubes) how to combine two such numbers, combining the 5s and then joining the 'bits left over'. For example: $(5 + 3)+(5 + 2)= (5 + 5)+(3 + 2)=15$.
- Repeat the work, this time (if appropriate) using lengths of towers beyond 10 – breaking them into '10 and a bit' or '15 and a bit'.

Paired work
- Present the twelve pieces, on card, from photocopiable page 69. Fold along each centre fold to form self-standing cards. Arrange these so that the number sentences are facing away from the children.
- Remind the children about the idea of partitioning into tens and units or '5 and a bit'. Each child takes turns to throw the two dice (see 'You will need' above). They must identify the numbers and match them to the folded cards. Turn the cards around to display the numbers' partitioned equivalent.
- Challenge the children to work out the total of the two cards, by adding the multiples of 5 or 10 from each card and then adding the 'bits' left over. For example: $(10 + 3)+(5 + 2) = (10 + 5)+(3 + 2)$.

Plenary
- Look at the largest total achieved and how its components were partitioned and recombined. Record the stages formally.

Potential difficulties	Further support
The dice may potentially give totals which are beyond the child's capability/experience.	Modify the cards and dice to smaller numbers. For example, two identical dice labelled 5, 6, 6, 7, 7, 8 require supporting cards 5, 6, 7 and 8 only.
Some may find it difficult to partition and recombine mentally.	Make the towers of interlocking cubes (used for demonstration during group work) available to the children during individual work.

Moving On
- Extend to include addition of larger numbers (such as: 21, 23 and 26).

Break it down

18	17	16	15
15 + 3	15 + 2	15 + 1	15
13	12	11	10
10 + 3	10 + 2	10 + 1	10
8	7	6	5
5 + 3	5 + 2	5 + 1	5

More than double

Learning Objectives
(Y2) Identify near doubles, using doubles already known (e.g. 8 + 9, 40 + 41).
(Y3) Identify near doubles, using doubles already known (e.g. 80 + 81).

Mental Starter
See the starter activity, 'Ten-times table' on page 17.

You will need
Photocopiable page 71 (one per child); practical apparatus for calculating doubles (such as base-10 apparatus, cubes or money); a prepared dice for each lighthouse panel (first lighthouse: 2, 4, 6, 8, 10, 12; second lighthouse: 5, 8, 10, 12, 15, 20; 3rd lighthouse: 20, 25, 30, 35, 40, 45); counters.

Whole class work
● Look at doubles of multiples of 5 such as 35. Use the knowledge of double 35 to establish answers to 34 + 35 and 35 + 36.
● Present a related (near double) problem such as 39 + 40, asking what would be a useful double to use in the solving of this problem.
● Repeat this for other numbers which are not multiples of 5 and 10 (for example 23 + 24).

Group work
● Revise knowledge of doubles to sample the range of numbers judged to be appropriate. Look at strategies for doubling numbers reliably:
  - counting on the same amount from the number being doubled.
  - using partitioning techniques (see 'Break it down', Lesson 21).
  - emphasising that all doubles of whole numbers must be even.
● Look at near doubles (such as 8 + 9) by doubling the first number in the sentence and adding one to that amount. Use some of the numbers from photocopiable sheet (page 71) to find out if the children are capable of the paired activity below. If difficulty is anticipated or experienced at this stage, the task should be simplified (see Potential difficulties/Further support below).

Paired work
● Photocopiable page 71 provides a choice of three graded tasks on the theme of near doubles. Cut out a lighthouse panel for each child (according to ability, the children do not need to have the same one) and give them the appropriately labelled dice (see 'You will need').
● The children take turns to roll the dice and must double that number to identify the 'near double' depicted on the game board. Offer additional materials for support (such as base 10 apparatus, cubes or money). If the appropriate number is vacant on the lighthouse grid, it can be claimed with a counter. Play proceeds until all the numbers are claimed.

Plenary
● Review the tasks in terms of techniques employed and those calculations which proved more difficult.
● Consider playing a whole group version of the task, with yourself acting as a caller and children using peer support to check each other's claims to specific near doubles.

Potential difficulties	Further support
The concept of a near double may be problematic when taught in isolation.	Consider modifying the grids to represent doubles only.
The range of numbers, even on the 'easiest' panel, may be too great.	Use a standard dice to find the appropriate numbers on a modified panel (a lighthouse labelled 2, 4, 6, 8, 10, 12).

Moving On
● Extend the range of near doubles, including totals both one more *and* one less than a given double.

More than double

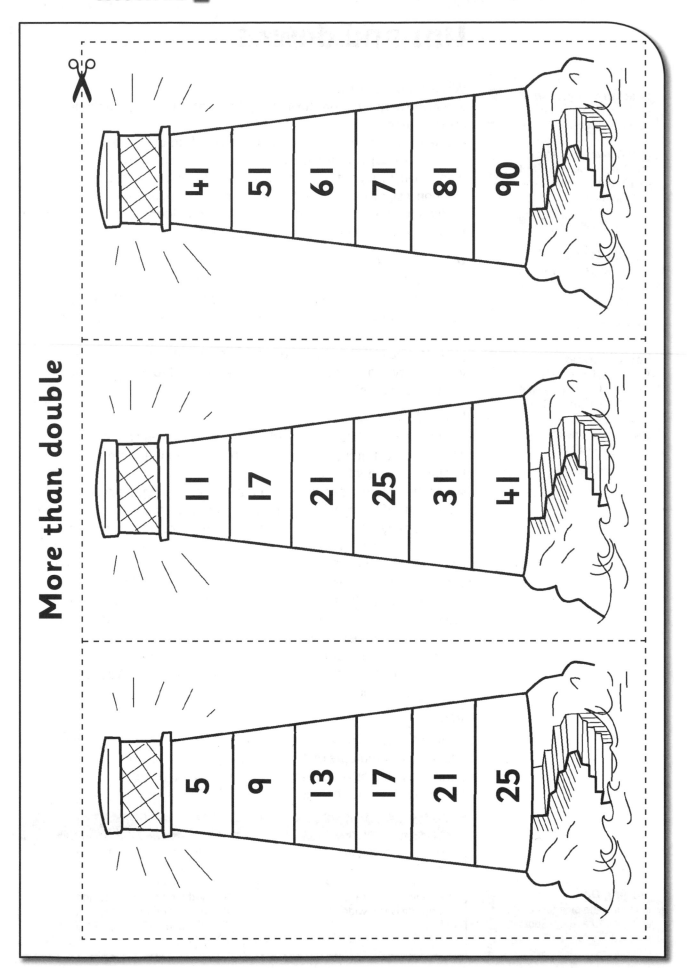

41	51	61	71	81	90

11	17	21	25	31	41

5	9	13	17	21	25

Ups and downs

Learning Objectives
(Y2) Add/subtract 9 or 11: add/subtract 10 and adjust by 1.
(Y3) Add and subtract mentally a 'near multiple of 10' to or from a two-digit number.

Mental Starter
See the starter activity, 'Halves and doubles' on page 17.

You will need
A dice labelled +9, +9, +10, +11, -9, -11; photocopiable page 73 (one per child/pair); counters; removable memo stickers; large number grid (0–99 or 1–100).

Whole class work
● Identify a number on the 100 square that is not located around the outside edge.
● Ask for a number that is 10 more and confirm the spatial location (directly below) of that answer. Use this arrangement to establish what 9 and then 11 more than the original would be, and stress again the positional significance. Do the same for 9 and 11 fewer.
● Use this spatial knowledge and visual aid to identify 9 or 11, more or fewer than any given number from the grid.

Group work
● Present a 0–99 or 1–100 grid and cover one of the numbers with a removable memo sticker. Ask: *What number is 10 more than this?* Do the same for other numbers and introduce the idea of numbers 10 less than a given number.
● Once it has been established that such questions require either a vertical move to the cell above or below, extend to 9 or 11, more or less than a given number.

Paired work
● Provide each child or pair with a copy of photocopiable page 73. Give each child a counter (in different colours if working together). Ask them to place their counters on 1 on the grid.
● Let the children take turns to roll the dice, moving the counter accordingly. If a player is at 1, they cannot move any further backwards.
● In the early stages the children should be encouraged to count on/back to find the next position, but they should begin to refer to the visual prompts provided on the sheet. Sometimes a player will be at the end of a row and consequently may not be able to make a diagonal move. Adding 11 (in such cases) can be taught as a vertical shift to the cell below (adding 10) followed by a further move of 1 (onto the left hand end of the next row).
● The dice has a positive bias towards addition which should ensure advancement down the grid as play progresses. Play concludes when a child goes beyond the end of the grid.

Plenary
● Discuss occasions where these skills might be useful (such as when adding a near multiple of 10 in shopping situations). Point out that items are often pitched just below a multiple of 10 to make them appear 'cheaper' to the unwary shopper!

Potential difficulties	Further support
Play takes too long to hold a child's attention.	The grid can be reduced to (say) 0–49.
The choice of operation and magnitude is too wide.	Modify the dice to include addition and subtraction of 10 and 11 only, (dice labelled +10, +10, +11, +11, -10, -11).

Moving On
● Modify the dice to include shifts of 19 and 21. Spot the pattern

Ups and downs

Subtract 9	Subtract 10	Subtract 11

Add 9	Add 10	Add 11

1	2	3	4	5	6	7	8	9	10
11	12	13	14	15	16	17	18	19	20
21	22	23	24	25	26	27	28	29	30
31	32	33	34	35	36	37	38	39	40
41	42	43	44	45	46	47	48	49	50
51	52	53	54	55	56	57	58	59	60
61	62	63	64	65	66	67	68	69	70
71	72	73	74	75	76	77	78	79	80
81	82	83	84	85	86	87	88	89	90
91	92	93	94	95	96	97	98	99	100

Spot the pattern

Learning Objectives
(Y2) Use patterns of similar calculations.
(Y3) Use patterns of similar calculations.

Mental Starter
See the starter activity, 'Number families' on page 17.

You will need
Photocopiable pages 63 and 75 (see the activity, 'Full score' on page 62).

Whole class work

● Provide a number sentence such as 46 + 54 = 100. At this stage you might discuss how there are 9 tens and 10 units in total.
● Write a related number sentence underneath by adding 10 to 46 and, in return, reducing 54 by the same amount. Double check that the compensation enables the total of 100 to be conserved.
● Invite the class to follow the pattern by adding to the sequence of number sentences. End the sequence when 96 + 4 is generated.
● Try another combination using numbers of a similar scale.

Group work

● Revise number bonds for a given number such as 12. Ask the children: *The total of two numbers is 12. What might those two numbers be?* Collect the suggestions as a series of number sentences, making links from one to another. For example, 5 + 7 may follow 6 + 6, (one lower, one higher).

Individual work

● Prepare the activity by cutting out cards 1 to 14 from page 63.
● Add totals to suit this range all the way down the right-hand column of boxes on photocopiable page 75. Explain that you would like the child to find a pattern of solutions for the given total. So, for a target of 15, suitable pairings would include 14 and 1; 13 and 2 and so on.
● For this example, arrange the prepared set of number cards from photocopiable page 63, in a line from 1–14 (ascending order) in front of the child. Begin by taking the smallest number from the line and recording that on the first space of photocopiable page 75. Remind the children that the total they are trying to make is 15. To complete the calculation, the number 14 must be selected to form a complementary pair. Confirm that this makes the target total using counting on methods (with suitable visual prompts such as a number line).
● The task proceeds with further removal of numbers from the extreme ends of the line of remaining cards. Some children may begin to offer an insight into why the pairings conserve the total. Continue the pattern on the reverse of the sheet if required.

Plenary

● Discuss how many different number sentences there are for bonds of 10, beginning with 5 + 5. As this is modified 'outwards', you may decide to include 0 + 10 and 10 + 0, giving 11 possible solutions.

Moving On
● Work with a range of numbers beyond those suggested above and/or start with minimum values above one - for example, work with the range 15 to 25 to make totals of 40.

Potential difficulties	Further support
Some children may follow the spatial pattern without recognising the numerical significance.	If available, a number balance (or similiar) can be used to reinforce the sense of equilibrium.
The idea of *conservation of number* may not be appreciated	Provide trays with the appropriate number of objects (the target number). Progressively shift one object each time from one side to the other.

Spot the pattern

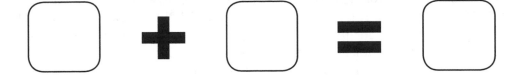

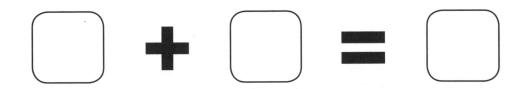

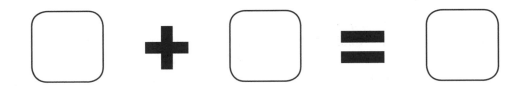

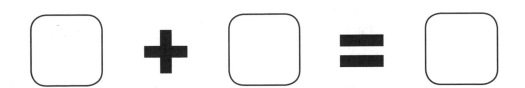

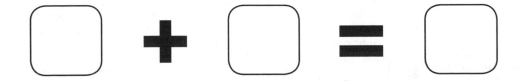

How much?

Learning Objectives
(Y2) Use known number facts and place value to add/subtract mentally.
(Y3) Use known number facts and place value to add/subtract mentally.

Mental Starter
See the starter activity, 'Number families (2)' on page 18.

You will need
Base-10 apparatus (or 10p and 1p coins); photocopiable page 77 (one copy per pair).

Whole class work

● Present two numbers for addition featuring unit digits greater than 5 (for example 47 + 39). Separate both numbers into tens and units.
● Begin by adding the 40 and 30, these being the most significant elements in terms of size. Add the two units which, owing to their size, require quick recall of numbers greater than 10.
● Combine the two sub-totals to give the answer. Invite individuals to solve other combinations of numbers.

Group work

● Engage the children in counting in tens, both forwards and backwards to check that the counting order is secure. Provide some of the numbers featured on photocopiable page 77; asking individuals to model these numbers physically with base-10 materials.
● Move on to combining two numbers, chosen not to require any 'carry-over' (exchange) with the tens. Explain that the tens from each number are combined, as are the units. Record the totals as a number sentence.
● Finally, select numbers where exchange is necessary. Group as before and, where there are more than nine units, ten of these must be exchanged for a ten to present the number in its 'simplest' form. Record the outcomes as in the following example:

$$45 + 27 = 40 + 5 + 20 + 7 = 60 + 12 = 72$$

Paired work

● Explain that, working in pairs, the children are going to find totals of two numbers, using base-10 materials (or similar) as demonstrated.
● Prepare the number cards by cutting out page 71 (ideally backed/printed on card). Place these face down (randomly scattered). Ask each child to select one of these, helping them to say the number. Support individuals in creating that amount using tens and ones.
● Now ask each child to record the two numbers selected in the form of a number sentence for addition. Use the apparatus, grouping tens first, to combine the two sets and therefore find the total. Be clear to use mathematical language which is familiar to the children.

Plenary

● Review the results obtained and try to establish which combination gave the highest total. Reinforce the steps involved in partitioning and combining two given numbers.

Moving On
● Encourage the children to mentally calculate the totals of the tens and then the units, prior to checking by counting.

Potential difficulties	Further support
Some children may experience difficulties in combining tens and ones, particularly where some combinations create totals where the units exceed 9.	Modify the activity sheet to include numbers where the combination of units will not exceed 9.
When counting the tens, some children may count them accurately but, for example, report this total as *six* rather than *six tens* or *sixty*.	Encourage children to count out verbally in tens.

How much?

16	45	32	24
31	27	56	12
38	57	44	54

Windows

Learning Objectives
(Y2) Understand the operation of multiplication as repeated addition or as describing an array.
(Y3) Understand multiplication as repeated addition. Read and begin to write the related vocabulary. Extend understanding that multiplication can be done in any order.

Mental Starter
See the starter activity, 'Make that 10' on page 18.

You will need
Photocopiable page 79 (one per child); large objects for describing arrays of 12; counters.

Whole class work
● Draw six 'matchstick' people and ask for the total number of legs between them. Discuss how the answer could be arrived at - by counting, by doubling the number of people, by counting in twos, and so on. Record the calculation formally as 2 times 6. Next, draw five four-legged creatures and discuss how the answer of 20 legs was calculated. Record the calculation as 4 times 5.
● Invite the children to draw sketches using other creatures (for example spiders, starfish) and to discuss such problems.

Group work
● Begin by showing an array of eight, using two rows of four large objects. Ask the children how many they can see and how the objects are arranged. Steer the discussion to include the vocabulary of rows and columns, demonstrating how the array can be described as two sets of four – or from another perspective, four sets of two.
● Invite the group to show how 12 objects might be arranged to form a rectangular array. At each point, record the arrangement as a number sentence. Given the commutative nature of multiplication, an array can be recorded either way without any ambiguity (for example, a 6 by 2 array can correctly be written as $2 \times 6 = 12$ or $6 \times 2 = 12$). Other possible solutions include $3 \times 4 = 12$ and $1 \times 12 = 12$.

Paired work
● Provide pairs with photocopiable page 79 and a supply of counters. Invite them to explore arrays for themselves with either 12 counters or any another number with several factors (such as 16 or 20).
● When two or more solutions have been found for any given number, invite the children to cut out representations of these arrangements to form suitably-sized arrays of smiley faces. These could be described as 'smiley faces at the window'.

Plenary
● Review some of the arrays produced and guide each child to stick their arrays onto paper and then write the appropriate number sentence next to or below it. Reinforce the commutative nature of multiplication (in everyday terminology).

Moving On
● Show the children that numbers such as eleven cannot be arranged, other than as one single line of counters/smiley faces. Although this is a later idea, such an observation prepares for work on *prime* numbers.
● Work with a greater number of counters than suggested earlier.

Potential difficulties	Further support
The language of multiplication may be unfamiliar so it should not be assumed that related terminology will automatically be understood.	Offer visual prompts (such as word banks) for newly introduced terminology.
Some children may not appreciate that each row should feature the same number of objects, with extra items incorrectly being 'squeezed' onto one or more rows.	Arrange a large grid under the counters to ensure that spacing is regular and windows are rectangular.

Name _____

Windows

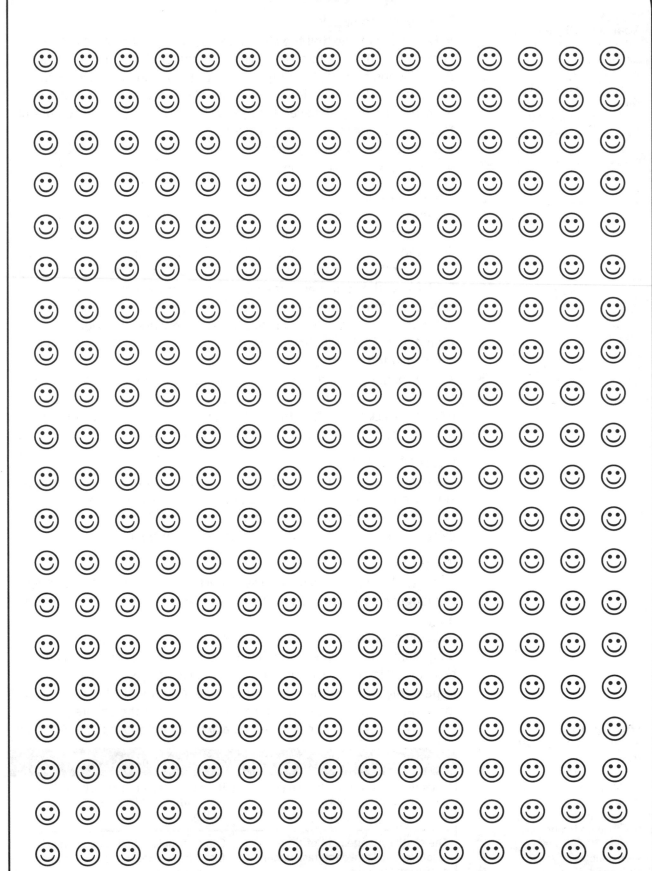

Double trouble

Learning Objectives
(Y2) Know and use halving as the inverse of doubling.
(Y3) Recognise that division is the inverse of multiplication, and that halving is the inverse of doubling.

Mental Starter
See the starter activity, 'Make it 20' on page 18.

You will need
Photocopiable page 81 (one per child); cubes for counting; basic (non-scientific) calculators (optional, as detailed under 'Plenary' below).

Whole class work

● Beginning at one, tell the class that you are going to double the number lots of times to make it 'grow'. As the doubles progress to 2, 4, 8, 16, 32 and beyond, target questions to those individuals who are likely to be able to calculate these amounts. Extend as far as possible.
● By moving through several stages of this challenge it will be possible to sample a range of calculation strategies.
● Without the use of any recorded prompts, repeatedly halve the number to return back to one.

Group work

● Revise knowledge of doubles of numbers, initially in the range one to ten. Extend beyond this if appropriate. Link the idea of halving to doubling, explaining that one operation can 'undo' the other.
● Cut out the left-hand half of the activity sheet as one large rectangle. Fold across the centre with the detail facing outwards. Fold again to isolate 8, again to show 4, again to show 2 and then once more to show 1. By reopening each fold, it is possible to show how 1 doubles to 2, then 4, 8 and 16. Note how at each successive stage, the numeral is supplemented by the appropriate number of dots.
● Use counting objects such as a tower of 16 interlocking cubes. Show how 16 is halved to form two equal towers of 8 which can then be reformed back again. Ask the children to use the cubes to continue halving down to one and then doubling back to 16.

Individual work

● Provide each child with a copy of the empty grid from the right-hand side of the sheet and ask them to begin with a low starting number such as three. Offer as much support as required to create a grid and calculate the numbers required at each stage of doubling.

Plenary

● Invite the children to take turns to perform their use of the grid. Note the language that they use as this will offer a valuable assessment of progress.
● Some calculators (typically non-scientific versions) can be programmed to repeatedly double a given number (although this must be checked in advance). Enter 1 X 2 = to give an answer of 2. Repeatedly pressing the = key without clearing the display each time may double that number. Try the same with any of the children's starting numbers to 'check' the accuracy of their doubling (3 x 2 = = ...).

Moving On
● Work with larger start numbers.
● Create more stages of doubling using larger sheets of paper.
● Where doubling has taken the children to numbers beyond 20, consider how such doubles might be calculated mentally.

Potential difficulties	Further support
Sometimes the idea of doubling is mistakenly interpreted as adding on 2.	Resist any temptation by the child to work without objects as a visual model.
The spatial arrangement of the resource could make the task unduly confusing for some.	Create doubling chains in graphical forms (for example, a staircase of 1, 2, 4, 8, ... steps).

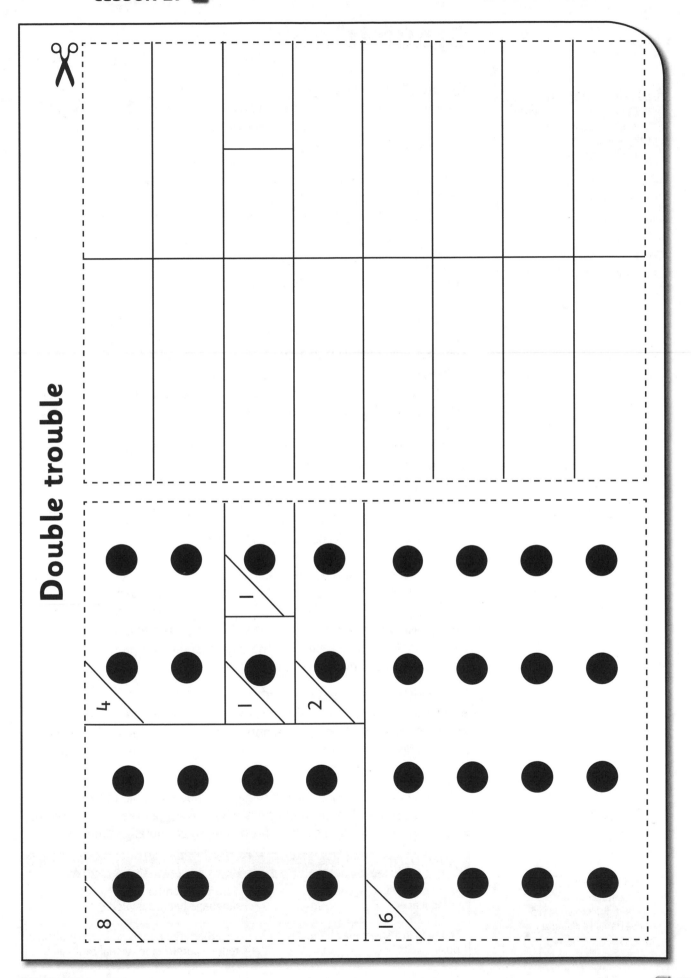

Double trouble

Group it

Learning Objectives
(Y2) Count on/back from/to 0 in different size steps.
(Y3) Understand division as grouping (repeated subtraction) or sharing. Read and begin to write the related vocabulary.

Mental Starter
See the starter activity, 'Money box' on page 19.

You will need
Giant coins or base-10 for modelling; table charts and/or number grids; photocopiable page 83.

Whole class work
• Explain to the class that a child has 60p to share with a friend. Model the situation using giant coins or similar to establish how much each child would get. Stress the importance, in this case, of equal shares as this is generally implied if a disproportionate split is not stated.
• Introduce the idea of a third child being included in the share and identify the resulting split (such as 20p each).
• Extend to sharing between 4, 5 and 6 as 60p has many factors.

Group work
• Recall the multiplication facts in order for the 3-, 4- and/or 5-times table. Make use of demonstration materials such as tables, charts and number grids.
• Provide a pot of 12 items and ask for these objects to be counted. Count them back in by counting back, making sure the first object is dropped in audibly as '12' (not 11). Now ask the children to remove three counters from the pot and count the remaining objects (9).
• Now refer the children to photocopiable page 83, where the top panel includes four clusters of three beads, making 12. Reinforce that the illustration also shows that three less than 12 is nine. Remove three further cubes and refer the children back to the illustration as before. Continue this process down to zero.
• As the children work, ask related questions such as:
  - With what number did we start?
  - How many did we subtract each time?
  - How many threes did we subtract?
  - How many threes make 12?
• Now model the activity with the 12 objects again, this time removing four at a time. Refer to the middle panel of the activity sheet.
• Finally, provide the children with eight more objects to give a total of 20 and ask them to remove four at a time and then five at a time. These two examples can be related to the middle and lower panels (respectively) on the photocopiable sheet.

Individual work/paired work
• Prepare some simple challenges based on removing a given number of cubes each time from a collection of objects. Decide on the form of presentation and recording in accordance with the group's capability.

Plenary
• Review the work covered and begin to model suitable methods of recording some of the calculations (such as using pictures and/or words).
• Only use the division symbol if it has been previously sampled.

Moving On
• Introduce some calculations which leave some items remaining at the end.

Potential difficulties	Further support
Some of the language may be unfamiliar.	Carefully monitor the range of language being sampled.
The resource sheet may be too 'busy'.	Use the three panels separately to reduce potential for visual confusion.

Group it

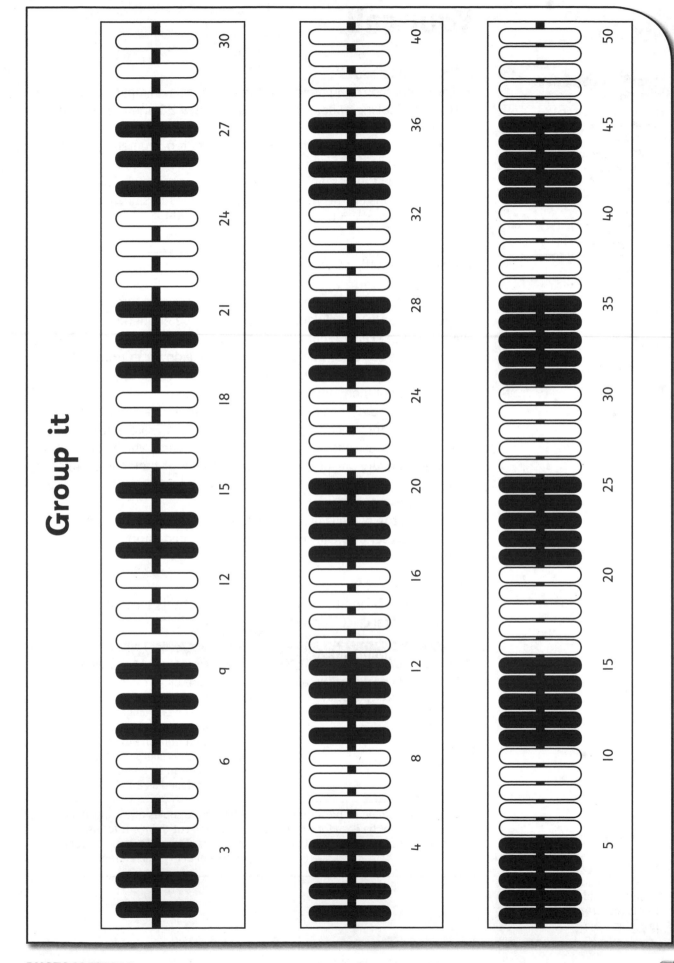

Your call

Learning Objectives
(Y2) Count on in twos from and back to zero or any small number.
(Y3) Know by heart multiplication facts for the two-times table.

Mental Starter
See the starter activity, 'Top numbers' on page 19.

You will need
Counting stick; photocopiable page 83.

Whole class work
● Revise doubles of numbers, with the emphasis on rapid recall.
● Begin by looking at doubles to a maximum of 20 and then beyond (if appropriate).
● Use a counting stick (with divisions to form ten segments) to count out the two-times tables in sequence from 0 to 20 (these being represented by the beginning and end of the apparatus). Point to specific divisions on the stick and invite the class to say what that position represents in terms of the two-times table.

Group work
● Model the multiples of two using familiar visual models (such as counting beads).
● Copy photocopiable page 85 onto card and cut into three individual 'bingo cards' and 12 individual cards. This will be enough for three players and the caller (yourself or a child).
● Shuffle the call cards and scatter them, face down, in front of the caller. Provide each player with a bingo card and some counters for covering the solutions for the statements called.
● Call out the cards, selected randomly, one at a time. Note that one of these is 2 X 0 for which no players can claim. This will provide an opportunity for discussion. There is also a 'star card' which acts as a free go, whereby every player can cover any number of their choice, but only if they can say an appropriate number sentence to match the number that they choose.
● Although the game is won when a player has covered all the numbers, further play can continue to give a satisfactory conclusion for everyone.

Plenary
● Return to recalling the two-times tables, but this time begin to look for some mental calculation strategies.

Potential difficulties	Further support
The mental calculations may cause particular difficulty or delay.	Modify the 'bingo cards' to include the number sentence associated with each given number. The child will still be required to do a mental conversion from one to the other (for example, the caller's statement 'two times three' must be matched to the square detailed as 2 X 3).
Having the statements presented verbally may not be easy for visual learners to retain that information.	Make extra copies of the individual cards and cut them out for use as counters. This will provide players with a direct visual reference.

Moving On
● Produce bingo cards featuring a mixture of the 2-, 5- and 10-times tables – or an even wider range of tables restricted to totals less than (say) 25.

Name _____

Your call

		20
14		10
8		6
	4	

2 multiplied by 5	★	2 times 9	2 times 10
6 sets of 2	2 x 0	2 times 3	Double 7
8 groups of 2	1 set of 2	2 multiplied by 2	4 groups of 2

16		
	10	
8		6
	2	4

	18	20
12		
6		8
		2

Find a partner

Learning Objectives
(Y2) Count on in steps of 5.
(Y3) Know by heart multiplication facts for the five-times table.

Mental Starter
See the starter activity, 'Make it up (2)' on page 19.

You will need
Counting stick; counting materials (for example, interlocking cubes); photocopiable page 87.

Whole class work
● Use a counting stick (with divisions to form ten segments) to count out the five-times tables in sequence from 0 to 50 (these being represented by the beginning and end of the apparatus). Point to specific divisions on the stick and invite the class to say what that position represents in terms of the five-times table.

Group work
● Model the multiples of five using familiar visual models (such as interlocking cubes grouped in fives).
● Next, ask the children questions that will encourage them to use the facts that they know to generate an answer. For example, if a child knows that 5 X 6 = 30 then he or she may reason that 5 X 7 will be five more).

Paired work
● Prepare photocopiable page 87 by cutting out the 20 cards. Shuffle the cards and place them face down in four rows of five.
● Invite the children to take turns to pick any two cards in an attempt to find a number story with an equivalent solution. If the cards do not match, they must be turned back over in their original positions. All attempts can be used as a vehicle for discussion and, when appropriate, the children can use practical equipment to support their work.
● When the children make a successful pairing they may retain the cards – the objective being to finish with the most cards.

Plenary
● Provide some word problems where the multiplication fact must be derived from the interpretation of the question. For example, ask: *How many sides will five pentagons have?*
● Discuss the multiple of five which results in an outcome of zero (5 X 0). Ask the children to try to explain this in their own words.

Potential difficulties	Further support
Some children may need further reinforcement of counting in fives, despite the cards featuring visual depictions of multiples of five.	Provide visual prompts (such as a 100-square) to offer further support.
The statements extend beyond the child's comprehension or experience.	Reduce the resource set to just 12 cards (5 X 1 to 5 X 6) with solutions.

Moving On
● Create additional pairings (5 X 0 and 0; 5 X 11 and 55; 5 X 12 and 60).

Find a partner

✂

5 x 3	25	5 x 8	50
10	5 x 5	35	5 x 10
5 x 2	20	5 x 7	45
5	5 x 4	30	5 x 9
5 x 1	15	5 x 6	40

www.scholastic.co.uk

50 MATHS LESSONS · AGES 7-9

Links

Learning Objectives
(Y2) Count on in steps of 3, 4 or 5 to at least 30, from and back to zero.
(Y3) Begin to know the three- and four-times tables.

Mental Starter
See the starter activity, 'Countdown' on page 20.

You will need
Counting stick; cubes or number lines; photocopiable page 89.

Whole class work
● Use a counting stick (with divisions to form ten segments) to count out the three-times tables in sequence from 0 to 30 (these being represented by the beginning and end of the apparatus). Point to specific divisions on the stick and invite the class to say what that position represents in terms of the three-times table. Repeat the above for the four-times table.

Group work
● Count from zero in steps of three. Demonstrate (with cubes or number lines) the use of practical/visual calculation methods (repeated addition).
● Repeat the above for steps of four and then steps of five. For the latter, reinforce the repetitive nature of the unit digit (alternates between zero and five).
● Prepare the activity sheet by copying onto card and cutting all 24 pieces along the dotted lines. Shuffle and share the pieces out.
● Proceed as with a game of conventional dominoes. Any player can start, as the pieces are created as part of a 'continuous loop'. A new piece must align diagonal to diagonal, or square edge to square edge.
● Use each turn as an opportunity to discuss the given calculation or target number, making use of practical counting aids (such as cubes or number lines).
● If a player is unable to use any pieces, play passes to the next child. If played competitively, the winner is the first person to use all their pieces. The varying combinations mean that the loop could end before all counters are placed; in this case, the winner is the person with the least pieces. Note that when all pieces are correctly played, both end pieces will match (thus completing the 'loop').

Plenary
● Review the playing pieces to identify which numbers are represented more than once (such as 24). Such numbers have several factors and could lead to further work on the lines of the activity 'Windows' on page 78.

Potential difficulties	Further support
Some may find the idea of 3 x 0 = 0 somewhat complex as it is often assumed that 'something' must arise out of multiplication.	Use a tower of cubes to represent 3 x 3, 3 x 2 and 3 x 1 (with the tower getting progressively smaller). Removal of the final tower models 3 x 0.
Some larger products may cause significant difficulty or delay.	Reduce the number of 'domino' pieces and create a similar activity using (say) products no greater than 20.
The pieces do not give enough contextual/visual information.	Enlarge the resource sheet to A3 to use visual arrays. Alongside the answer 15, for example, five rows of three dots could be drawn as a visual prompt for the required piece (5 x 3).

Moving On
● Produce a variation of this activity using a wider range of multiplication facts.

Links

25	20	10	15	27	16
18	15	30	4	24	3
3 × 6	3 × 5	5 × 6	4 × 1	4 × 6	3 × 1
4 × 3	4 × 7	3 × 8	3 × 0	3 × 10	3 × 7
12	28	24	0	30	21
5	9	20	8	6	12
5 × 1	3 × 3	4 × 5	4 × 2	3 × 2	3 × 4
4 × 4	5 × 5	5 × 4	5 × 2	5 × 3	3 × 9

Seeing double

Learning Objectives
(Y2) Derive quickly doubles of all numbers to at least 15 (for example, 11 + 11 or 11 x 2).
(Y3) Derive quickly doubles of all whole numbers to at least 20 (for example, 17 + 17 or 17 x 2).

Mental Starter
See the starter activity, 'What's my number? (1)' on page 20.

You will need
Photocopiable page 91; base-10 materials (if required); interlocking cubes; small mirrors.

Whole class work
● Provide flashcards featuring numbers (or simply write these on the board) for the children to double. Begin with numbers to ten, extending to 20 and possibly beyond. With some of the 'harder' doubles, discuss the strategies used. In some cases the number will determine the strategy (for example, double 19 might be considered double 20, less 2).
● Express a double in the form of repeated addition (for example, 17 + 17) and as the operation of multiplication (for example, 17 times 2).

Group work
● Look at the concept of doubling by taking a ten's piece and a small number of units. Hold a mirror to this set and count how many can be 'seen' altogether as a form of doubles. Represent the initial quantity in written form, partitioned as a ten and a number of units. Duplicate the same numbers directly underneath, to explore double the quantity. This is established by adding the tens together, then adding the units and, finally, combining these sub-totals. For example, to double 12:

$$
\begin{array}{ccc}
10 & + & 2 \\
10 & + & 2 \\
\hline
20 & + & 4 & = & 24
\end{array}
$$

● Repeat the process, with a number in the range of 16 to 19, as this could be seen as '10 and 5 and a bit'. Model with interlocking cubes organised by colour in strips of five with one or more 'extra' cubes of another colour. When this is duplicated, the strips of five and ten can be matched for ease of counting.

Individual work
● Provide each child with a small mirror and a copy of photocopiable page 91 cut into 12 separate tiles. Work through each of these numbers, explaining how they are all based on multiples of 5 and the idea of '5 and a bit'.
● Ask each child to select one card and to match that number with base-10 materials. In order to double this amount, they must take the same amount again and combine.

Plenary
● As a form of reinforcement, a mirror can be used directly across their cards to represent each double.
● To consolidate the work, demonstrate the stages of practical partitioning as a formal algorithm (see the example in 'Group work', above).

Moving On
● Provide additional cards featuring numbers beyond the given range. Encourage the children using the cards to find the doubles mentally.

Potential difficulties	Further support
The numbers may be too large to enable access to the task.	Modify the sheet to feature numbers in the range (say) from 1 to 12 only.
The method of partitioning is too abstract.	Find doubles using single cubes only, duplicating a given number and 'counting all' in ones.

Seeing double

7	8	9
▭▭▭▭▭ 5 ▭▭ 2	▭▭▭▭▭ 5 ▭▭▭ 3	▭▭▭▭▭ 5 ▭▭▭▭ 4
11	12	13
▭▭▭▭▭▭▭▭▭▭ 10 ▭ 1	▭▭▭▭▭▭▭▭▭▭ 10 ▭▭ 2	▭▭▭▭▭▭▭▭▭▭ 10 ▭▭▭ 3
14	15	16
▭▭▭▭▭▭▭▭▭▭ 10 ▭▭▭▭ 4	▭▭▭▭▭▭▭▭▭▭ 10 ▭▭▭▭▭ 5	▭▭▭▭▭▭▭▭▭▭ 10 ▭▭▭▭▭ 5 ▭ 1
17	18	19
▭▭▭▭▭▭▭▭▭▭ 10 ▭▭▭▭▭ 5 ▭▭ 2	▭▭▭▭▭▭▭▭▭▭ 10 ▭▭▭▭▭ 5 ▭▭▭ 3	▭▭▭▭▭▭▭▭▭▭ 10 ▭▭▭▭▭ 5 ▭▭▭▭ 4

Double vision

Learning Objectives
(Y2) Derive quickly doubles of multiples of 5 to 50 (for example, 20 x 2 or 35 x 2).
(Y3) Derive quickly doubles of multiples of 5 to 100 (for example, 75 x 2, 90 x 2).

Mental Starter
See the starter activity, 'What's my number? (2)' on page 20.

You will need
Counting apparatus featuring tens and fives (for example, giant coins); photocopiable page 93.

Whole class work
● Provide some giant 10p and 5p coins. Create a scenario where an amount of money is doubled by winning a competition. Explain that one way of doing this is to 'match' that amount with an identical set of coins.
● Model this exercise for 35p and invite individuals to do the same with a different amount (featuring a multiple of 5). Stress the idea of grouping the tens together, adding this (if applicable) to the ten pence created from the two 5p coins. Choose a small amount (for example 25p) and invite an individual to explain (in words alone) for others to visualise.

Group work
● Revise counting in tens and then counting in fives. Sample a range of such multiples up to 50.
● Next, present such multiples as isolated numbers and ask for a number which is double in value. Ask: *How did you calculate that answer?*. Explore strategies used, including the partitioning of numbers into tens and units. In cases where the number ends in 5, the double will involve combining that digit with itself – leading to an answer ending in zero.

Paired work
● Provide each child with a copy of photocopiable page 93 (cut into sections – the dial and the five individual pieces).
● Ask each child to take a turn to roll both dice and to collect the appropriate pieces. Tell the child to use their 'number wheel' to place the sections around the arc, starting from the top and heading clockwise. The sections will end with an appropriate reading on the scale (representing the total of both amounts).
● Now ask the child to work out what double that number would be and how the answer was calculated. The result can be checked by sliding the first piece ahead of the second and then the second piece ahead of the first. Alternatively, you might simply provide two identical pieces to add to the wheel.

Plenary
● Start with some of the doubles achieved above and ask the children to give the number with half that value. Confirm how halving can 'undo' doubling and share strategies for calculation.

Potential difficulties	Further support
The circular dial may be too complex for some children to understand.	Some children may require a linear number track. This could be created using labelled rods (of unit length 5, 10, 20, 30, 40) and a prepared track.
The range of numbers may be too great.	Modify both the dial, the dice and the value of the pieces to generate smaller totals (and corresponding doubles).

Moving On
● Modify both the dial, the dice and the value of the pieces to generate larger totals (and corresponding doubles).

Double vision

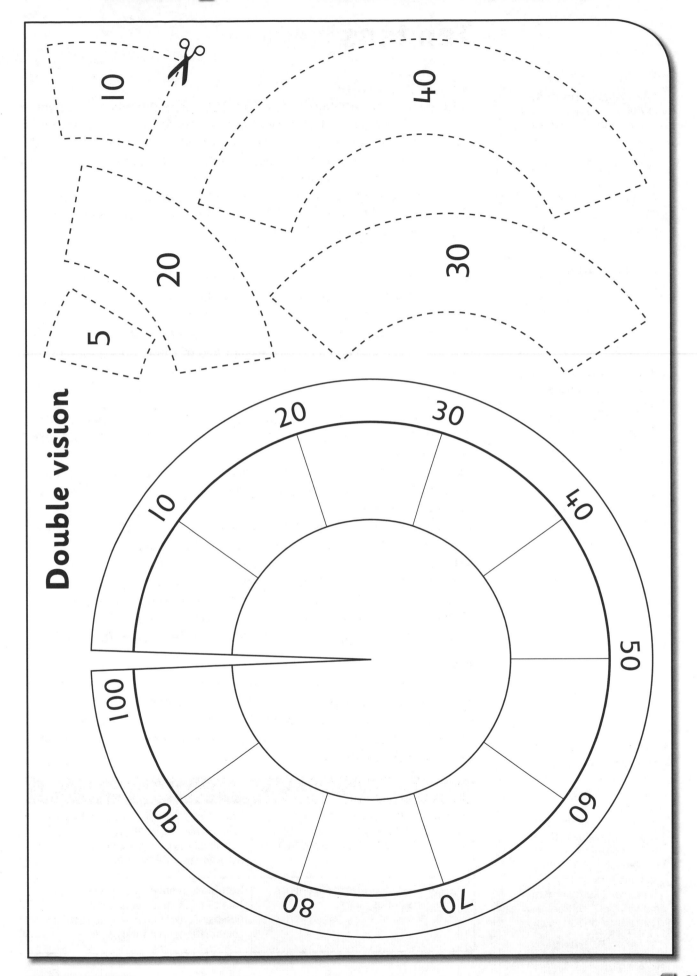

Ten tens

Learning Objectives
(Y2) Know by heart all pairs of multiples of 10 with a total of 100 (such as 30 + 70).
(Y3) Derive quickly all pairs of multiples of 5 with a total of 100 (such as 35 + 65).

Mental Starter
See the starter activity, 'What's my number? (3)' on page 21.

You will need
Photocopiable page 95 (one copy per pair); a demonstration 1-100 square.

Whole class work
● Begin with the statement 50 + 50 = 100. Write the related problem 45 + _ = 100 underneath this, inviting the class to calculate or reason the missing number. If necessary discuss the idea of compensation and explain how the two number sentences inter-relate. Continue the sequence to create several number sentences.
● Highlight the way the numbers leading to a total of 100 have tens digits which add to either 9 or 10. In the former cases, the 9 tens (or 90) is 'made up' by the addition of the units.

Group work
● Practise counting in tens by tracking down the final column of a demonstration 1-100 square. Select a multiple of 10 (such as 40) and engage the children in counting on in tens from that number up to 100 (60 more). Try other examples, reinforcing the idea that we start with a multiple of ten and add on a further multiple of ten to give a total of ten tens.

Paired work
● Provide each pair of children with a copy of the activity sheet (page 95), cut out to give ten pieces. These can be spread out face down. Ask each child to select one of the pieces and, in turn, ask how many tens they have and how many more tens are needed to make ten tens (100). Each child proceeds in turn by taking a second tile which they feel will take the total up to 100. (Note that the tiles are proportional in size to the quantity they represent. The tiles also depict rows of ten dots so that a successful pairing will give ten rows of ten dots.)
● Continue selecting tiles to find matching pairs, encouraging the children to offer mutual support when appropriate.
● When all five pairings are found, glue them together on separate pieces of paper and add the appropriate number statements alongside each one (for example: 3 tens and 7 tens = 10 tens; 30 + 70 = 100).

Plenary
● Provide related number sentences involving subtraction from 100 (for example, 100 – 40). Use the learning from the above activity to make links between addition and subtraction. This section will also help the children to recognise how a knowledge of complementary pairs can be useful in such situations.

Moving On
● Provide extra copies of the sheet and encourage individuals to find combinations of three tiles to give a total of 100. Can they find the one combination of four tiles giving a total of 100?
● Provide extra tiles with multiples of 5 to give pairs with a total of 100 (such as 95 + 5 = 100).

Potential difficulties	Further support
The visual array of dots and the proportional quality of the cards do not aid calculation for some children.	Produce a card template to represent 100. A child experiencing difficulties can simply overlay two pieces to identify suitable pairings.
The child has insufficient experience of numbers in this range.	Return to complementary pairs with totals of 10/20 or reduce the number of existing pieces to restrict combinations to a total of 50.

Ten tens

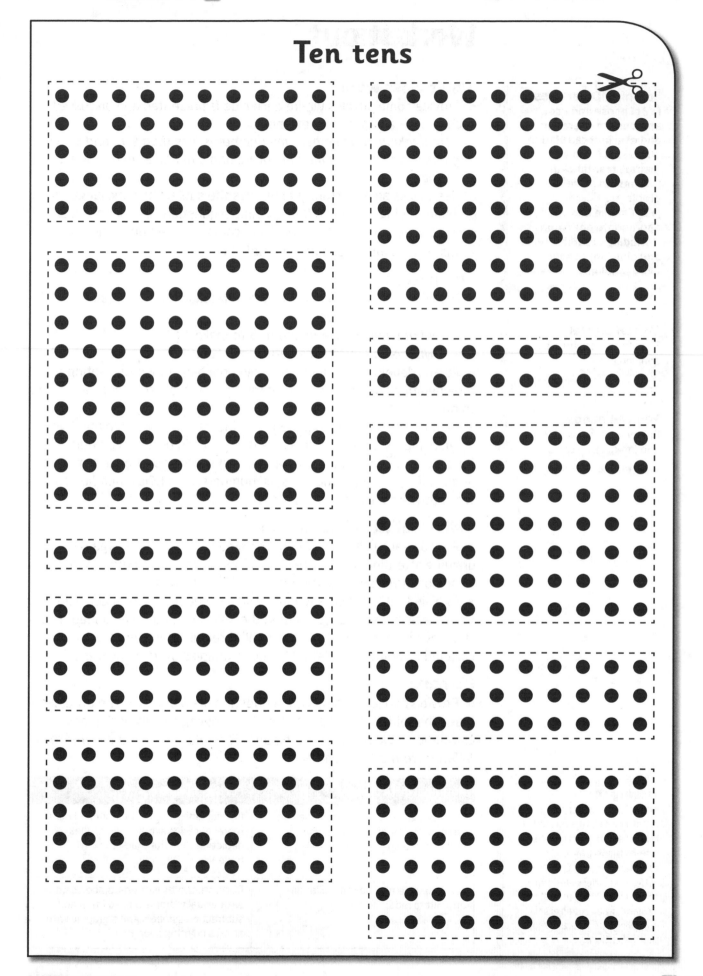

Work it out

Whole class work

- Provide some puzzles where each clue is presented and discussed at each of several stages. For example:
  - *I'm thinking of a number… my number is less than 90… and greater than 40… is a multiple of 5… and a multiple of 10… and a multiple of 3.* (Answer 60)
- Use this as an opportunity to discuss the subject specific language of problem solving. Provide relatively simple questions sampling words such as *more, less* and *between*. More complex questions could consider terms such as *multiple of* and *divisible by*.

Group work:

- Provide some questions verbally of the following type/scale:
  - *What is 13 subtract 4?*
  - *What would I have to add to 6 to make 11?*
  - *What is the difference between 12 and 7?*
- As you develop each question, build up a bank of words relating to the operations of addition and subtraction, such as, *sum, difference*, and so on.
- Develop questions to explore the numbers lying between any two given numbers. Show the idea as either two odd or two even numbers (to ensure the answer is a whole number) spaced apart on an empty number line, adding in the 'missing' numbers. Ask: *Which number is half way between these two numbers?*.

Individual work/paired work:

- Provide each child or pair with the nine cards cut from page 97, drawing attention to how the pieces 'jigsaw' together. Form a sentence to demonstrate, such as: *the total of …12 and … 4 is … .*
- Explain that the task is to make and copy number sentences made from these cards. After calculation the answer can then be added. The challenge is for children to attempt all three different types of calculation, and to complete different examples by 'mix and match'.

Plenary:

- Provide two large cards with a question mark on each. The other side hides the solutions 4 and 9. Write the following for discussion and calculation: *Two numbers are hidden. The total is 13. The difference is 5. What are the two numbers?*

Learning Objectives

(Y2) Choose and use appropriate operations and efficient calculation strategies (such as mental, mental with jottings) to solve problems.
(Y3) Choose and use appropriate operations (including multiplication and division) to solve word problems.

Mental Starter

See starter activity 'Next door' on page 21.

You will need:

Photocopiable page 97 cut into interlocking cards.

Moving On

- Provide a wider range of numbers (taking care not to mix odd and even numbers when calculating the number half way between) Introduce a new card with the words "The product of". Provide small numbers if sampling the operation of multiplication.

Potential difficulties	Further support
The number halfway between may be wrongly identified as any number within the range.	Reinforce the use of the number line or represent with actual number tiles depicting the entire range under review.
The language may be unfamiliar or difficult to read.	Decorate the three 'non-number' cards with visual prompts (i.e. addition and subtraction symbols and a graphic with arrows pointing inwardly).

Work it out

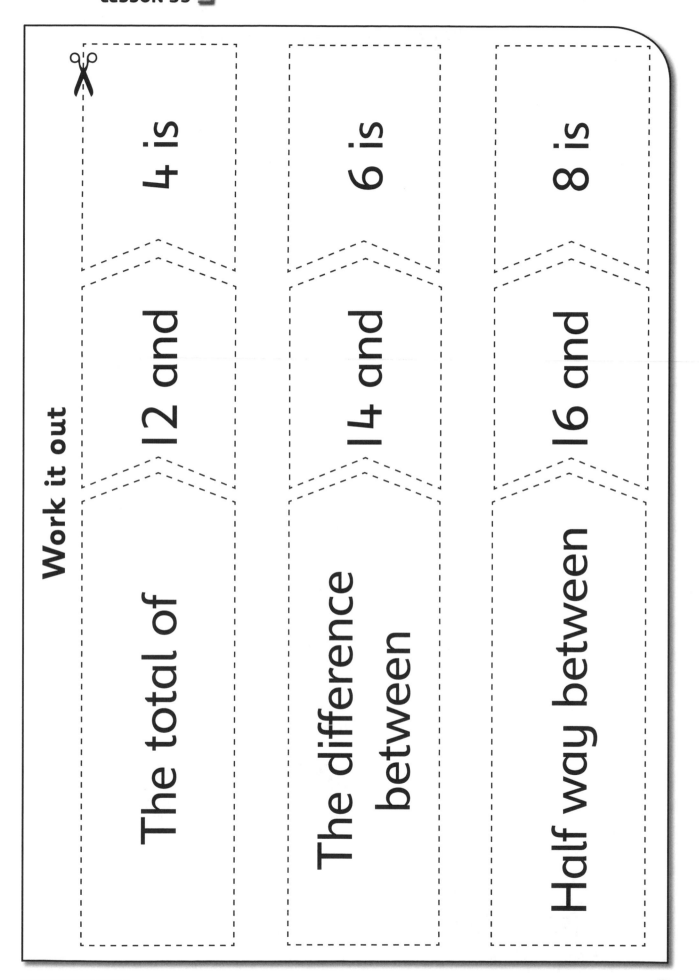

4 is

12 and

The total of

6 is

14 and

The difference between

8 is

16 and

Half way between

Pictures and words

Learning Objectives
(Y2) Choose and use appropriate operations and efficient calculation strategies (such as mental, mental with jottings) to solve problems.
(Y3) Choose and use appropriate operations (including multiplication and division) to solve word problems.

Mental Starter
See the starter activity, 'Halve it' on page 21.

You will need
Photocopiable page 99; real objects and pots for counting.

Whole class work
● Present a range of number problems in words, linked by the operation of multiplication. Include examples involving repeated sets (for example, *if one car has 4 wheels, how many wheels will 6 cars have?*) as well as scaling (for example, *I have 6p but I need 4 times that amount to buy a bar of chocolate. How much is my bar of chocolate?*).
● For all examples discuss strategies for calculation. In some cases instant recall is an acceptable 'method'. Other strategies include 'doubling twice' a given number to find four times that amount, and repeated addition involving counting in the same step size.

Group work
● Show the children an example of how to visually represent a multiplication problem. For example, draw four triangles explaining that each of the four triangles has three sides. The number of sides is represented as 3 X 4 = 12 (three sides multiplied by four) and this number sentence should be given.
● Present a picture of three pentagons and ask the group to construct a similar word sentence about the number of sides. Identify how this could be represented as a number sentence.
● Provide a few more examples, generated from 'real life' and repeat the process.

Individual work
● Provide each child with a copy of photocopiable page 99. Three of the boxes feature partially completed representations. The problem given in words is typically the most accessible. The final (blank) panel is designed for individuals to create their own problem and then represent it in all three ways (words, picture and number sentence).
● Real objects and pots can be used to model the problem in a physical way. Be prepared to support individuals as the needs arise.

Plenary
● Compare the children's examples and refine the language as necessary. Address the issue of *commutativity* in an accessible way (for example, show how three pots each containing four flowers gives an equivalent number of flowers to four pots each containing three flowers).

Moving On
● Introduce division as an *inverse* of multiplication, viewing items as being shared into two or more subsets (for example, 12 flowers shared by four people gives each person three flowers).

Potential difficulties	Further support
Some children may find the representation of problems in written or symbolic form particularly difficult to interpret.	Read prepared word problems for re-interpretation in pictorial forms.
The resource sheet may look too 'busy' in its existing form.	Quarter the activity in advance in order to separate the four tasks.

Pictures and words

Picture:

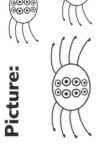

Words:

Number sentence:

Picture:

Words:

Number sentence:

Picture:

Words:
3 flowers in each of
the 4 vases.

Number sentence:

Picture:

Words:

Number sentence:
6 x 2 = 12

Squares in squares

Learning Objectives
(Y2) Solve mathematical problems or puzzles, recognise simple patterns and relationships, generalise and predict. Suggest extensions by asking *What if...?* or *What could I try next?*.
(Y3) Solve mathematical problems or puzzles, recognise simple patterns and relationships, generalise and predict. Suggest extensions by asking *What if...?*.

Mental Starter
See the starter activity, 'Double it' on page 22.

You will need
Photocopiable page 101.

Whole class work
● Present a real chessboard and ask the children to suggest the total number of squares. Typically the answer of 64 squares will be given. Show this, demonstrating how each square is of the same size and how each square is defining by having sides of the same length. Describe the 64 squares as 8 rows of 8, 8 columns of 8, or an 8 by 8 array.
● Ask the children whether the whole of the board is a square and, if so, why it should be counted as an 'extra' square in the count. Invite children to identify other squares (for example, 2 by 2).

Group work
● Provide a large representation of a 2 x 2 grid and invite children to openly describe what they can see (such as four squares; lots of lines; verticals and horizontals; joins). Offer suitable prompts if necessary.
● Steer the discussion to the observation of the squares. Establish (through prompts) that there are, in fact, five squares in a 2 x 2 grid if the perimeter is included as an additional (larger) square. Ask related questions which encourage further visual discrimination, such as: *How many rectangles can you see?*

Individual work
● Prepare by cutting the various pieces from page 101. Start by providing each child with the left-hand side of the photocopiable sheet, showing the 3 x 3 grid. Provide each child with the 3 x 3 grid and ask them to count the squares. Typically, a child will say, 'nine', or, if the earlier teaching has been assimilated – 'ten' to include the large square which forms the perimeter.
● Now give each child the small (single) square and ask them to position it in all possible places on the big square, counting how many positions it can occupy (nine). Repeat the process with the medium square (this can be placed in four places). Finally, ask them to position the large square (which can only fit in one position). Make a total of all the positions (14). Explain that this is the number of squares contained in the grid.

Plenary
● Work together with the children to look at the number of squares on a 4 x 4 grid. Encourage systematic ways of working. At this stage the actual solution is perhaps less important than the process skills being nurtured. (There are 30 squares in a 4 X 4 grid.)

Potential difficulties	Further support
The level of spatial/visual discrimination may be too complex for some children.	Provide interlocking cubes and simply explore the number required to make a 2 x 2 square (4), 3 x 3 square (9) and so on.
The placing of the 2 x 2 square may seem quite random and all possibilities may not be found.	Encourage a systematic approach (starting top left, sliding right, then down and across to bottom left).

Moving On
● Extend the task to investigating an equilateral triangle generated from nine smaller equilateral triangles.

Squares in squares

How many squares can you count?

How many ways?

Whole class work

- Arrange five cubes on a flat surface to create a solid shape (each cube attached to at least one other cube). If an overhead projector is available, the resultant shape can be shown as a solid shadow.
- Invite children to create lots of different shapes to form simple sticks, L-shapes, and so on. Include discussion of whether some new shapes are no more than rotations of previously generated shapes. Other shapes may be 'flipped' versions of earlier examples.

Group work

- Provide each child with five interlocking cubes and ask them to make a 'flat' shape to place on the table. Use this opportunity to compare the different arrangements. Reinforce the importance of 'flat' shapes, (as the 'footprint' left by that shape is what will ultimately be recorded).
- Invite individuals to sketch the outline of the shape created. If two shapes are identical but are simply orientated differently, the *congruence* can be demonstrated by rotating one shape onto the other shape. Similarly you may have a discussion if one shape appears to be a 'flipped' version (reflection) of the other. (Allow a 'generous' definition of congruence, as the objective of this task is to look for patterns and to ask questions.)

Individual work

- Provide each child with a copy of photocopiable page 103. The spacing between the dots has been designed to accommodate a standard size of interlocking cube. If these fit, the shapes themselves can be laid on paper and used as a template.
- Ask the children questions that encourage prediction and/or mathematical description. For example, ask: *How many ways do you think you will find?; Would we make a different shape if we moved this cube to a different position?; Why is that shape different to that one?*

Plenary

- Draw the group together to review all the different shapes created. See if any individuals have found an example which others have missed.

Potential difficulties	Further support
Visual discrimination may be insufficiently developed to recognise when a seemingly different outcome is actually a rotation of an earlier example.	Keep each arrangement as they are created, in order to enable direct comparison.
The three-dimensional nature of the cubes confuses some children and they try to build upwards out of the surface.	Work with cut-out squares.

Learning Objectives

(Y2) Solve mathematical problems or puzzles, recognise simple patterns and relationships, generalise and predict. Suggest extensions by asking *What if...?* or *What could I try next?*.
(Y3) Solve mathematical problems or puzzles, recognise simple patterns and relationships, generalise and predict. Suggest extensions by asking *What if...?*.

Mental Starter

See the starter activity, 'More doubles' on page 22.

You will need

Interlocking cubes; photocopiable page 103; overhead projection (optional);

Moving On

- Extend the task by looking for combinations using six cubes each time.
- Consider how many symmetrical shapes can be made from six cubes.

How many ways?

How many different shapes can you make with 4 cubes?

Tower blocks

Mental Starter
See the starter activity, 'Money box (2)' on page 22.

You will need:
Photocopiable page 105; interlocking cubes in red and blue; red and blue coloured pencils.

Whole class work
● Provide the digits 1, 2, 3 and 4 and ask for a number 'in the thousands' using each digit once only (for example 4231). Reinforce the place value significance of each digit used in that number.
● Ask the class to 'fix' that first digit and to find further numbers with the remaining digits. There should be six possible combinations for a four-digit number with a common thousands digit.
● Explain that there are lots more combinations to be found by exchanging the first digit and fixing these as before (there are 24 possible combinations in total). Explain that lots of questions of this type require careful thought and systematic working.

Group work
● Begin by asking each child to take two cubes from a pile containing just two colours, and to form a short tower from them. Gather these examples together to see if all four unique combinations have been sampled. Discuss the idea of reversals being different, and the fact that some examples are made from just a single colour. Consider together how all four items can be sub-divided into two pairs of towers – each tower a 'colour inverse' of its 'partner'.

Individual work
● Provide each child with a copy of photocopiable page 105 which features towers made from three cubes. Begin by creating the two completed towers illustrated at the top of the sheet. (The size of the towers has been designed to accommodate a standard size of interlocking cube. If these fit, the shapes themselves can simply be laid directly on top of the illustrations.)
● Provide each child with sufficient cubes to enable the sheet to be completed. Use coloured pencils for permanent recording. The sheet provides the opportunity for all eight combinations to be found.

Plenary
● Ask individuals to identify the opposite pairs (inverses). Ask about the strategies the children used and how they know that all solutions have been found.

Moving On
● Provide three different colours and explain that each colour must be used in each tower. There are six unique combinations.

Potential difficulties	Further support
The number of different combinations may be too great, particularly for children lacking confidence in more 'open' tasks.	Provide a modified sheet with four towers of two units height. Repeat the task used in the *group work* section, but use different colours.
Some children may find the idea of one colour being the inverse of another too difficult.	This is not an essential outcome of the task, although an awareness of such qualities can often help find a 'missing' combination in problems of this type.

Name _____

Tower blocks

Here are two towers to colour. If you can only use red and blue cubes, make some different towers.

blue	red	blue

red	red	red

Building blocks

Learning Objectives
(Y2) Solve mathematical problems or puzzles, recognise simple patterns and relationships, generalise and predict. Suggest extensions by asking *What if...?* or *What could I try next?*.
(Y3) Solve mathematical problems or puzzles, recognise simple patterns and relationships, generalise and predict. Suggest extensions by asking *What if...?*.

Mental Starter
See the starter activity, 'Monkey puzzle' on page 23.

You will need:
Photocopiable page 107; large square tiles (card); counters/cubes (optional).

Whole class work
● Make a large copy of an empty tower (similar to that shown on page 107), adding an extra layer of four cubes on the base.
● Provide the numbers 1, 2, 3 and 4 on the base from left to right, and demonstrate how cells in the layers above are progressively filled with the totals from the two cells beneath. The top cell should be occupied with the number 20.
● Provide an identical tower but this time arrange the digits 1 to 4 on the bottom layer in a different order. Explore which variations lead to the highest and lowest totals.

Group work
● Revise 'instant' recall of number bonds to ten.
● Prepare some large square tiles of card to construct a tower in the way depicted on the worksheet. Build the tower, step-by-step, beginning with the base squares and labelling them as shown in the top left example on photocopiable page 107. Add the second tier of squares.
● Explain that the numbers on this tier are gained by adding the numbers on the base tier (3 + 3 = 6 and 3 + 1 = 4). The top square, producing a total of 10, is calculated in the same way.
● Generate a second tower, this time beginning with 10 at the top and progressively working backwards with suitable combinations. Ask the children: *What numbers might there be in these two middle spaces?*.

Individual work
● Provide each child with a copy of photocopiable page 107 and some cubes or counters. Explain that you would like them to continue the work with the towers, and that they must try to find some different solutions to the 'puzzles'.
● Support individuals as required. The task can be made more accessible by placing a tower of ten cubes at the top of the square. This can then be partioned across the middle section. Make further partitions to generate the bottom row, with the bottom right-hand cell calculated by visually observing how much needs to be added to the adjacent square to give the total above.

Plenary
● Look to see if individuals have found solutions different to the others. Have any children used 'zero'?

Potential difficulties	Further support
Working backwards from the top total proves too difficult or confusing.	Provide a modified sheet where the base numbers are given as opposed to the top total. These can be engineered to give a total of ten in each case, providing the procedure is carried through reliably.
The number of possible solutions could be seen as daunting.	Work with top numbers less than ten.

Moving On
● Work with numbers other than ten at the top and/or add an extra layer of four cubes on the base.

Name _____

Building blocks

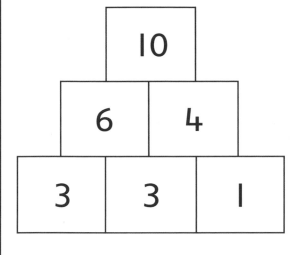

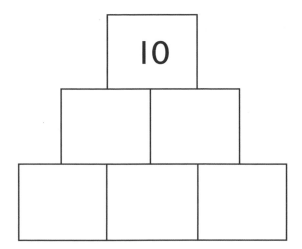

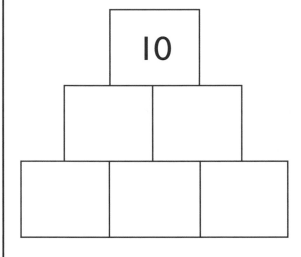

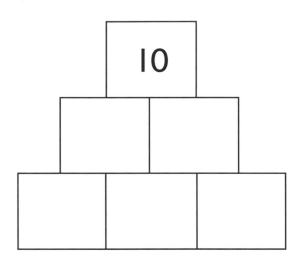

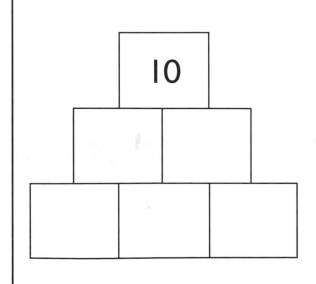

www.scholastic.co.uk

Up and away

Learning Objectives
(Y2) Explain how a problem was solved orally and, where appropriate, in writing.
(Y3) Explain methods and reasoning orally and, where appropriate, in writing.

Mental Starter
See the starter activity, 'Number families (3)' on page 23.

You will need
Photocopiable page 109 (one copy per child); large number tiles 1-6 (demonstration set); glue.

Whole class work
● Present the number 100 in a circle. Radiate a number of 'legs' from the circumference of the circle to create a spider diagram.
● Invite the children to give you an addition number sentence with the answer of 100. Encourage the class to derive new examples by adjusting/modifying earlier ones. Move to sentences involving subtraction. Encourage individuals to explain methods and to reason.
● Consider 'simple' multiplication facts that could lead to strategies such as 'doubling and halving' (for example knowing that 50 times 2 equals 100 could lead to 25 times 4 having the same outcome).

Group work
● Present the number tiles in a random order and ask the group to help you find the total. Invite individuals to choose two numbers to combine in order to begin the calculation (such as: 4 and 6 makes 10).
● Continue adding the remaining numbers to give a total of 21. Ask: *Will it give a different answer if we add them in a different order?* Try out some different orders to demonstrate how the total is 'conserved'.

Individual work
● Provide each child with some glue, pencils and a copy of page 109 (the upper section and the cut-out numeral cards from the lower section). Read the instructions together, ensuring that all the children are familiar with the term 'total'. Explain that they may need to 'trial and improve' before they get the correct solution.
● When a solution has been found, encourage each child to identify any specific strategies that were used, such as:
- matching numbers at the 'extremes'
- working to a specific total and realising that it is too large/small for others pairs to be created
- finding the total of all the numbers (21) and recognising that these have to be shared between 3 groups

Plenary
● The correct solution gives a total of seven in each balloon. Relate this back to the 'group work' where a total of 21 was calculated.
● Extend this initial activity, incorporating additional tiles to cover the range 1–8. Place the tiles in ascending order and explore the idea of matching totals by drawing from the outside extremes (1 and 8) through to 4 and 5. Establish that the total is equivalent to 4 groups of 9.

Moving On
● Consider modifying the sheet to include larger numbers. Any such set can be created by establishing a start number and adding on in regular steps. For example: 2, 4, 6, 8, 10, 12 or 2, 5, 8, 11, 14, 17.

Potential difficulties	Further support
The task is insufficiently visual.	Provide differently-coloured towers featuring 1, 2, 3, 4, 5 and 6 cubes. This will offer a valuable visual reinforcement of the solution when the towers are appropriately paired.
Individuals can sometimes be reluctant or unable to declare their strategies for problem solving.	Observe the child engaging in the task, providing a related activity if this was missed first time.

Up and away

- Put 2 numbers in each balloon. Each balloon must have the **same** total.
- How did you work it out?

| 1 | 2 | 3 | 4 | 5 | 6 |

Mix and match

Whole class work

● Prepare a fast food menu with items labelled 48p, 56p, 58p and 46p. The challenge is to select three of these items in order to spend exactly £1.50.

● Provide individual whiteboards (one between two) and/or guide them through 'attack' strategies which include: (a) 'Trial and improvement' to add 3 items; (b) the unit digits could be examined to see which combination leads to a multiple of 10p (thus ensuring that the resultant unit digit matches that of the target total); (c) each amount is centred above or below 50p by a relatively small amount. By looking at how much each item is above or below, these can be 'balanced' to give the correct combination.

Group work

● Combine two, two-digit numbers (giving similar examples to those given on photocopiable page 111) using base-10 materials, giant coins or real coins. Encourage strategies such as dealing with the most significant digits first (the tens). If coins are used, help the children to look for the largest denomination possible within that figure.

Individual work

● Give each child a copy of photocopiable page 111 and make a range and quantity of coins available. Read the challenge to the children and explain that the answer will not be immediately obvious. 'Trial and improvement' may be required (there are ten different combinations featuring three numbers with only the combination of 17p, 26p and 33p giving the required total).

● When a solution has been found encourage each child to identify any specific strategies that were used, such as:
  - 'fixing' two numbers and trying each one of the other numbers to see if this is successful
  - looking first at the units only (to give totals which align with the units tally in the number 76).

● Discuss the strategies with the children and help each child to answer the question on the photocopiable page.

Plenary

● Compare the different strategies used. Look at the unsatisfactory solutions to identify how many *incorrect* combinations there are.

Learning Objectives
(Y2) Use mental addition and subtraction to solve simple word problems involving numbers in 'real life', money or measures, using one or two steps. **Explain how the problem was solved.**
(Y3) Solve word problems involving numbers in 'real life', money and measures, using one or more steps, including finding totals. **Explain how the problem was solved.**

Mental Starter
See the starter activity, 'Number families (4)' on page 23.

You will need
Photocopiable page 111 (one per child); 'giant' coins for demonstration (if available); quantity of real coins (range of denominations from 1p to 20p); individual whiteboards.

Moving On
● Create similar problems based on the notion of combining any three lengths of paper strip to make a given length.

Potential difficulties	Further support
The scale of the numbers may be problematic for some children, particularly as they are required to find the total of three numbers.	Modify the sheet to feature smaller numbers and/or a given total generated from the addition of two numbers only.
Individuals can sometimes be reluctant or unable to declare their strategies for problem solving.	Observe the child engaging in the task, providing a related activity if this was missed first time.

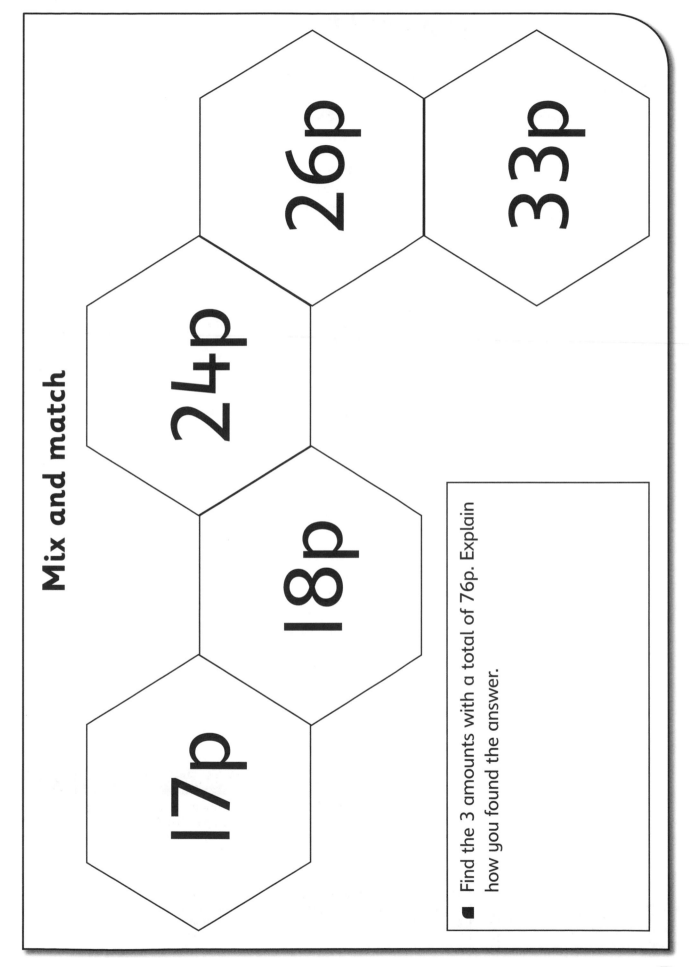

Mix and match

26p

33p

24p

18p

17p

■ Find the 3 amounts with a total of 76p. Explain how you found the answer.

How old?

Mental Starter
See the starter activity, 'Calculator patterns (3)' on page 24.

You will need
Photocopiable page 113 (one copy per individual) prepared as detailed under 'Individual work'; number line to 30; individual whiteboards.

Moving On
● Provide a similar scenario with the final card giving future projections. In the given example, the final clue could be modified to say, 'in 6 years, Richard will be *twice* as old as Ann'.
● Other scenarios can be created to sample the operation of addition (such as: 'Sue and Dylan have a combined age of 26 years').

Whole class work
● Provide a visual scenario of a mother and daughter aged 28 and 8 respectively. Project how old mother and daughter will be in 2, 4 and 5 years time, by adding equally to both ages. Present these as pairings, written underneath each caricature.
● Ask the class to discuss in small groups, using whiteboards, at what point the mother will be exactly twice as old as her daughter.
● Some children may want to explore their age in relation to their own family members, although this may need sensitive handling!

Group work
● Present two simple sketches of two children; one labelled 'Sara, age7', the other labelled 'Sam, age 5'. Invite individuals to make up statements linked to the idea of order and the operations of addition and subtraction. For example, 'Sam is younger than Sara'; 'Sara is two years older than Sam'; 'the difference in age is two years'; 'their ages add up to 12'. This process will help to prepare them for the work below.

Individual work:
● Separate photocopiable page 113 into seven separate sections (six 'clue' cards and one solutions grid).
● Begin by providing the picture of Ann. Ask the group to think about how old she *might* be, and avoid declaring her actual age. Next, present the card featuring Richard and, again, invite suggestions about the person's apparent age. The third and fourth cards offer information which establishes that Richard is Ann's elder brother.
● Now present the fifth card. This gives a further clue about their respective ages, by declaring the age *difference* of 12 years. Use this information to help the children re-evaluate their estimates.
● Now give the children the card that requires them to record some possible ages which retain the given age difference (such as 17 and five). When this is complete, provide the final clue card which, through examination and further calculation, should confirm that their ages are 18 and six.

Plenary
● Talk to the group about their siblings. Use the information to create some similar statements. Concentrate simply on the language (rather than trying to produce a fresh challenge).

Potential difficulties	Further support
The final clue card introduces the operation of multiplication which, alongside the concept of difference, may prove too complex.	Modify the card to declare, for example, that 'Ann is 6 years old'. As a result, reference back to the recorded suggestions will probably reveal the correct combination.
The task may be too abstract in nature or remote from personal experience.	Change the task completely to simply make 'fact cards' (with mathematical details about their own family).

How old?

This is Ann.

This is Richard.

Richard is older than Ann.

Richard is Ann's brother.

Richard is 12 years older than Ann.

How old might they be?

Richard	Ann

Final clue: Richard is 3 times older than Ann.

Big spender

Learning Objectives
(Y2) Use mental addition and subtraction to solve simple word problems involving money, using one or two steps. **Explain how the problem was solved.** **(Y3)** Solve word problems involving money using one or more steps.

Mental Starter
See the starter activity, 'Calculator patterns (4)' on page 24.

You will need
Photocopiable page 115 (one per pair or small group) prepared as detailed under 'Paired work'; 100 square or large number line; real money (a *closed* set of coins would feature £1, 20p, 20p, 20p, 10p, 10p, 10p, 5p, 2p, 2p, 1p coins – giving a total value of £2).

Moving On
● Develop additional scenario cards to feature further purchases. Expect children to find totals more readily (including mental approaches), and to use 'counting on' for giving change.

Whole class work

● Provide a number such as 36 and model counting on to 100 using an empty number line. Reinforce the idea of bridging through the next multiple of 10 and, in some cases, making use of other convenient staging posts (such as the 'jump' from 50 to 100). Explore an alternative approach involving counting in tens from the given number. The answer can then be found by counting in ones as 100 is approached.

● Both the approaches given above can be modelled on a 100 square.

● Relate the idea of counting on as a method for giving change. As time allows, model this with coins. Other skills can be incorporated here, such as the use of 20p to bridge from 30p to 50p, and the use of a range of denominations for giving the minimum number of coins.

Group work

● Revise making given totals (up to £1) from the coins provided. Reinforce the idea of making such amounts efficiently, by looking for the largest denomination possible within that figure.

● Combine any two piles of coins and look to see if such a total could be 'tidied' through exchange (to produce a minimal set).

Paired work

● Supply photocopiable page 115 pre-cut into eight sections. Spread the sections out in front of the two children.

● Explain that you would like them to solve this shopping problem which is given in words and pictures. All the clues are available to work out both how much is spent, and what money is left.

● Help the children to work through the cards, to make sense of all the information and to organise the data. It is important, for example, to recognise that not only were 'Twisties' 15p, but also that two were purchased.

● If you wish, model the task as if £1 was actually given as payment – requiring the total and change to be calculated (as in a 'real' shopping situation). Alternatively, exchange that coin for 20p, 20p, 20p, 10p, 10p, 10p, 5p, 2p, 2p and 1p. These lower denomination coins should enable items to be 'bought' individually. The remaining coins represent the 'change' from the original £1.

Plenary

● Revise giving change using counting on (sometimes referred to as 'shopkeepers' addition').

Potential difficulties	Further support
The amounts are too high for ease of calculation.	Modify the task to include items priced more cheaply with totals less than 50p.
The cards are too far from 'reality'.	Create simple shopping scenarios using real items (suitably labelled).

Big spender

I have £1 to spend.

I buy a comic.

What change do I get?

I buy two packs of Twislers.

Twislers cost 15p each.

I buy a packet of crisps.

How much?

Learning Objectives
(Y2) Recognise all coins and begin to use £.p notation for money (for example, know that £4.65 indicates £4 and 65p). Find totals, give change, and work out which coins to pay.
(Y3) Recognise all coins and notes. **Understand and use £.p notation** (for example, know that £3.06 is £3 and 6p).

Mental Starter
See the starter activity, 'Find a partner 1' on page 24.

You will need
Photocopiable page 117, prepared (one per child) as detailed under 'Individual work'; glue; plain paper; 'giant' demonstration coins (if available).

Whole class work
● Explore the equivalence of different coin denominations (for example five 20p coins have the same value as two 50p coins). Record these as written statements using the 'equals' symbol to illustrate equivalence.
● Provide some prepared questions of the type, *I have three coins with a total value of 32p. What are my coins?* This should support the class in making progressive use of the largest available coins to a given amount.

Group work
● Use 'giant' demonstration coins (if available) and revise making the amounts of each of the four items found on photocopiable page 117. Reinforce the idea of making such amounts efficiently, by looking for the largest denomination possible within that figure. Establish that such totals have been made using the *fewest* coins.

Individual work
● Prepare photocopiable page 117 by cutting out all 12 rectangles from the lower section of the sheet. The larger panel at the top may be used as a reference point throughout the task.
● Explain that the task is for the children to consider what two items they would buy, given a free choice. Let the children glue two of the pictures side-by-side as a 'purchase'. Next, ask the children if they can find further combinations of two different items each time. Completed successfully, six unique pairings will be found (using all of the available illustrations).

Plenary
● Help the children to find totals of all the 'pairings' that they made. Alternatively, ask the group to 'help' calculate the pairing with the *largest* total. Provide a large selection of coins to make the separate amounts in order to combine them. Finally, carry out any necessary exchange to 'tidy' the solution.

Potential difficulties	Further support
One pairing will give a total of £4.07 which some children may erroneously record as '£4.7'.	Clarify this convention, with reference to the importance of the zero as a place holder.
The cost of each item (and subsequent combinations) is too large.	Modify the amounts depicted on the photocopiable sheet.

Moving On
● Challenge the children to make combinations and totals where any *three* items can be purchased.

How much?

£1.73　　　　£1.22　　　　£2.85　　　　£1.05

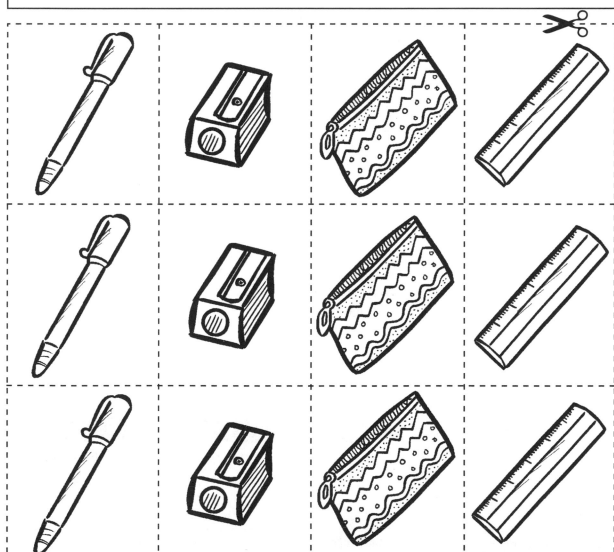

What's on?

Learning Objectives
(Y2) Solve a given problem by sorting, classifying and organising information in simple ways.
(Y3) Solve a given problem by organising and interpreting numerical data in simple lists, tables and graphs.

Mental Starter
See the starter activity, 'Find a partner (2)' on page 25.

You will need
Photocopiable page 119 (one per child); television listings from newspapers and magazines; glue; scissors; paper.

Whole class work
- Provide all or part of the class timetable for a 'typical' week. Ask specific questions such as when a particular session begins, days on which specific subjects are taught, lessons that feature each week day.
- Invite individuals to set questions of their own for the class to answer.
- Set a sequence of questions involving time differences (for example, the length of lunchtime). For periods a little above/below a whole number of hours, it is often helpful to move on in whole hours initially and to compensate forwards/backwards to the target time. To that end, a geared clock is a valuable teaching aid.

Group work
- Show the children examples of television listings. Ask them what information the listings give and how the information is organised.
- Let the children talk briefly about the types of programme they watch (genres, such as 'sport' rather than specific titles).

Individual work
- Present the simplified television listing depicted on photocopiable page 119 and briefly review the format across the three (fictional) channels. Ask the children to identify the programme types, leading to a list as follows: 'sport'; 'films'; 'cartoons'; 'news and weather'. Write the list as headings on a separate piece of paper.
- Using the above classifications, invite the children to cut out each programme as a rectangular block. Ask them to glue these 'blocks' under the appropriate headings listed on the sheet.
- When the children have finished, ask questions which require them to interpret the data, such as:
    - How many cartoons are there on that day?
    - Are there more sports programmes than films? If so, how many more?
- Then ask individuals to think of suitable questions based on the available information.
- Please note that as the listings will have been disassembled, it will not be possible to establish how long each programme lasts without reference to a fresh copy of photocopiable page 119.

Plenary
- Begin to look at the calculation of time differences by reviewing when a given programme starts and finishes.

Moving On
- Calculate how long each programme lasts and use this information to find the *total* viewing time for each category of programme. If appropriate, this data could be presented graphically through a suitable software application (such as a spreadsheet).

Potential difficulties	Further support
Organisation skills are poorly developed.	Prepare a 'collation sheet' in advance of the activity, labelled with the four categories of programme. Colour-code each heading and, as appropriate, each programme.
Reading capability hinders comprehension.	Offer one-to-one reading support.

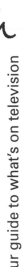

What's on?

The Box

Your guide to what's on television

Channel 1		Channel 2		Channel 3	
1.00pm	News National and International	1.30pm	Funzone USA Cartoon action from the Big Apple	12.30pm	News round up Lunchtime news and issues
1.30pm	Film Wanda the Wombat	2.00pm	Formula 1 Racing live from Bahrain	1.15pm	Afternoon cinema Classic movies each and every day
3.00pm	Cartoon crazy Includes Mad Meg	5.00pm	News All you need to know in your area	2.45pm	Cartoon fun! Fun-filled assortment of your favourite animations
3.30pm	Racing today Horse racing live from Ascot	5.15pm	Classic Toons The cartoons which started it all	3.15pm	Wimbledon Highlights of yesterday's tennis action
4.30pm	News and weather Includes local events	5.45pm	Weather watch 15 minutes of 'what's hot and where's not!'	4.15pm	News 15 15 minutes of news with subtitles
5.00pm	Sports update 30 minutes of results from today's games.				

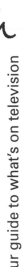

Days and months

Learning Objectives
(Y2) Use and begin to read the vocabulary related to time. Use units of time and know the relationships between them (second, minute, hour, day, week). **(Y3) Use units of time and know the relationships between them (second, minute, hour, day, week, month, year).**

Mental Starter
See the starter activity, 'Crossover' on page 25.

You will need
Photocopiable page 121 (one per child); 'month by month' calendars for the current year (various formats acceptable).

Whole class work
- Provide either an enlarged version of a month-by-month year planner or present the traditional poem, '30 Days has September … '.
- Ask specific questions for investigation such as, *How many days have the longest months?*, *Which month is the shortest?*.
- Identify when birthdays of people in the class occur, recording these against the appropriate months.
- Consider how two individuals may have birthdays in adjacent months and only be separated by one or two days. Use this as an opportunity to count days 'across the months'.

Group work
- Provide each child with a copy of photocopiable page 121 and shared access to current calendars from diaries, wall-mounted charts and so on.
- Ask the children to tell you what a month-by-month calendar details in terms of information. They could, for example, use the calendars to establish the day on which their own birthday falls in this calendar year.

Individual work
- Locate the current month on your example calendar and support the children in transferring the information to the left-hand side of their copy of the photocopiable page.
- Once completed, look at the patterns formed, such as the way each successive Monday is calculated by 'adding on 7' each time. (At this point, children may need to be referred to adjacent months to clarify why there may appear to be 'gaps' at the beginning and end of some months.)
- Work through the questions on the right-hand side of the sheet, working on each question with the whole group if necessary.

Plenary
- Look at further patterns in the array of numbers – for example, highlighting a block of four consecutive numbers in a square formation should give equal totals across its two diagonals. Look at similar patterns and relationships with a square of nine numbers.

Potential difficulties	Further support
The orientation of the calendar on the photocopiable page may vary from that on available calendars.	Modify the photocopiable page to more closely mirror the representations available.
The order and names of days may not be consolidated.	Modify the photocopiable page to include the days written out in full.

Moving On
- Teach the traditional poem, '30 Days has September … ' and see if the children can use this to establish the length of each month.
- Show calendars from previous years to demonstrate how birthdays 'float' in relation to the days on which they fall.

Days and months

- How many days in this month?

- How long is it to the end of this month?

- What will be the date this coming Saturday?

- On what day will the next month start?

- Find out which is the **shortest** month.

- What months have the **same** number of days as this month?

This month is _____

S	S	M	T	W	T	F

Shape jigsaws

Learning objectives
(Y2) Make and describe shapes, pictures and patterns using, for example, solid shapes, templates, pinboard and elastic bands, squared paper, a programmable robot.
(Y3) Make and describe shapes and patterns. For example, explore the different shapes that can be made from four cubes.

Mental Starter
See the starter activity, 'Number crunchers' on page 25.

You will need
Photocopiable page 123 (one per child); set of labelled 2D shapes (for reference).

Whole class work
● Create simple riddles or clues to help children recognise properties of different shapes.
● Explore the names of shapes that are less commonly referred to. These include heptagon (7 sides), nonagon (9 sides), decagon (10 sides).

Group work
● Revise the names of common shapes and discuss their properties:
- Rectangle – two pairs of parallel sides, right angles
- Square – two pairs of parallel sides, right angles and common lengths of side
- Parallelogram – two pairs of parallel sides
- Triangle – three-sided shape (include equilateral and right angled)
- Pentagon – five-sided shape
- Hexagon – six-sided shape.
● Please note that all polygons are defined as many sided shapes with straight sides.

Paired work
● Provide each pair with the ten triangles cut out from photocopiable page 123. Invite the children to work together to sort the triangles by type. (There are six equilateral triangles and four right-angled isosceles triangles in each set.) Both sets share a common length of side, although the hypotenuse of the latter is necessarily longer.
● Allow the children some time to arrange their shapes in different ways. Discuss the types and properties of the shapes created.
● Now direct the children towards specific tasks by taking one or more of the following suggestions:
- Use all four right-angled triangles each time to make a parallelogram, triangle, square, rectangle (oblong) and trapezium
- Use up to six equilateral triangles to make a rhombus, parallelogram, trapezium or hexagon.

Plenary
● Review the shapes created and then label them accordingly. Ask the children to explain which specific properties give the shapes their names.

Potential difficulties	Further support
Shapes cannot be formed without 'boundaries' to work within.	Provide templates of shapes to be created, suitably labelled with their names. Pieces can then be simply overlaid to cover these.
Visual discrimination and spatial awareness needs to be 'formally' recorded.	Provide multiple copies of the pieces so that shapes created can be glued down directly onto paper.

Moving On
● Ask about specific properties and establish if conservation of area is understood.

Shape jigsaws

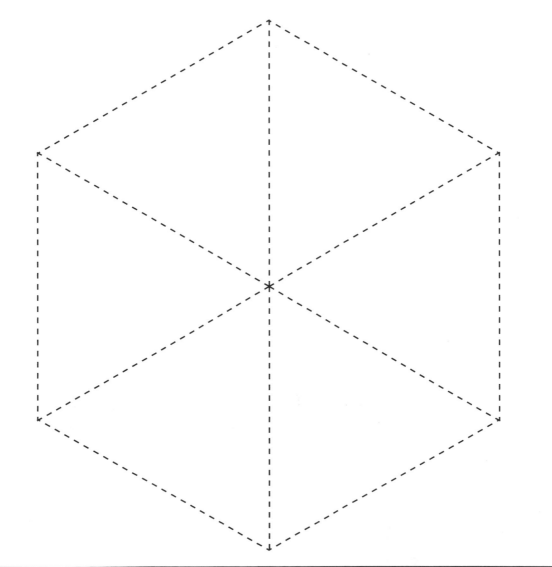

Mirror, mirror...

Learning Objectives
(Y2) Begin to recognise line symmetry.
(Y3) Identify and sketch lines of symmetry in simple shapes, and recognise shapes with no lines of symmetry.

Mental Starter
See the starter activity, 'Know your facts' on page 26.

You will need
A range of 'everyday' objects demonstrating symmetry; photocopiable page 125; small mirrors; interlocking cubes; overhead projector (optional).

Whole class work

● Ask the class what they understand by the word 'symmetry'. Ask them to recount previous work on the subject and/or examples of symmetry in the 'outside world'. If online access is available, review some examples of symmetry via a suitable search engine.
● Distinguish between the two types of symmetry (rotational and line).
● Explain that sometimes a shape may have both forms of symmetry or just one. Explain that the focus of work at this stage is mostly connected with line (reflective) symmetry.

Group work

● Present a range of objects or pictures of items with line symmetry. Talk about what makes such shapes symmetrical and identify the line of symmetry in each one. If the items detract from the 'footprint' they leave, or details within it 'spoil' the symmetry (such as the print on a credit card), then use an overhead projector to focus attention on the qualities of the projected (black) shape.
● As an alternative, create simple line drawings of images such as balloons, faces, butterflies and bottles to demonstrate horizontal/ vertical lines of symmetry.

Individual work

● Prepare several versions of the shape depicted on photocopiable page 125, using interlocking cubes of just one colour. Use a mirror to demonstrate how the shape is not symmetrical.
● Provide each child with a representation of the shape along with a further three loose cubes in a different colour. Ask them to add to the shape to make the new shape symmetrical (the colour is not a feature). In each case, a mirror needs to be placed along the line of symmetry to confirm that what is seen in the mirror matches what actually lies beyond it.
● Ask the children to draw a representation of the symmetrical shape they have made onto the photocopiable sheet, providing help where necessary. Encourage the children to find and make some more (fully connected) symmetrical shapes.

Plenary

● Together, draw up a 'complete' set of different symmetrical shapes.
● Demonstrate how an 'L-shape' made from five cubes, interestingly features a line of symmetry running diagonally through the corner cube.

Moving On
● Explore combinations for a different number of cubes.
● Turn attention to shapes which possess *rotational* symmetry.

Potential difficulties	Further support
Some children may be confused by the three-dimensional aspect of the shape, even though the focus is on its 'footprint'.	If the problem persists, the cubes can be replaced with card cut-outs.
Recording on the activity sheet is too difficult/unreliable.	Provide a continuous supply of cubes to allow the three-dimensional arrangements to be a record in themselves.

Mirror, mirror...

■ Add 3 more squares to make this shape symmetrical.

■ How many different ways can you find?

Angle-eater

Learning Objectives
(Y3) Identify right angles
in 2D shapes and the
environment.

Mental Starter
See the starter activity,
'What's the score?' on page
26.

You will need:
Photocopiable page 127; a
large square of card (for
demonstration).

Whole class work

● Talk to the children about three different types of angle (*acute, right* and *obtuse*) and provide examples of each.

● Draw some regular shapes and, within each, identify whether internal angles are acute, right or obtuse.

● If data projection is available, make use of software with angle estimation as a feature. The Interactive Teaching Programs (*National Numeracy Strategy*) feature suitable applications of angular measurement and are freely available online.

Group work

● Introduce the term right angle (some children may have been taught this as a 'square corner'). Provide both visual and kinaesthetic models of this:

Visual

Use a large square sheet of card with the corners marked with the right angle symbol in each corner. Overlay this in places such as table-tops or book corners and where a wall meets the floor.

Kinaesthetic

Explore the angle through which the door rotates about its hinges or engage the children in turning though a quarter turn.

Paired work

● This activity enables the children, working with a partner, to measure a static angle in a stimulating and active manner.

● Provide a pre-cut copy of the 'Angle-eater' from photocopiable page 127 and explain that its name comes from its ability to measure (eat) right angles. Demonstrate this by locating the mouth over the edge of a rectangular table-top. If the angle fits snugly in the mouth, then this means that a right angle has been found!

● Supervise the children as they work with a partner to find further examples of right angles in and around the classroom. Help them to use the remaining half of the sheet for recording successful finds.

Plenary

● Draw the group together to identify where right angles were found.

● Introduce some common shapes with right angles (such as rectangles and right angled triangles). Present some irregular shapes featuring right angles (such as a pentagon shaped like a house with a pointed roof).

Moving On
● Explore right angles using
a programmable vehicle
('floor turtle') or a computer
simulation of this. Some
vehicles allow angles to be
entered in degrees.

Potential difficulties	Further support
The term 'right angle' can sometimes be confused with 'rectangle'.	Present this as a potential (common) error in order to pre-empt problems.
Measurement is inaccurate.	Remind the group of the need for a good 'fit' with the angle eater (curved edges are not acceptable).

Angle-eater

I found right angles here.